Untangling IT
25 Years of Lessons in Effective IT Leadership

Robert S. Tipton

First Edition

Untangling IT
25 Years of Lessons in Effective IT Leadership

by Robert S. Tipton

Diva's Publishing
1041 W. Dry Creek Rd., Littleton, CO 80120-8012 USA

ISBN 0-9725674-0-2

Printed in the United States of America

Cover Art: Josh Aho

Edited by: Kathy Nelson

I am donating a portion of all profits from this book to:

The Adoption Exchange
14232 East Evans Avenue • Aurora, CO 80014
800.451.5246 • www.adoptex.com

- And -

DestiNation Imagination • South Metro • Colorado
7567 South Depew Street, Littleton, CO   80128
www.extremecreativity.org/smetro
www.DestiNationImagination.org

Untangling IT

Acknowledgments

*T*hank you to everyone with whom I have had the chance to work over the past 25 years — from my early mentors and teachers to my clients, partners, and team members. Without your wisdom, wacky antics, bizarre requests, and demanding attitudes, I wouldn't have had the chance to explore and discover just what it means to be an effective IT leader.

Thank you also to Debi, Amanda, Parker, Spencer and Grace for all of your love, patience, and support throughout the years. Special thanks to Trevor Perry for helping me to see the bird inside the egg related to this project in particular.

Introduction: Reality on a Bun

*J*ust what is this "Reality on a Bun" thing anyway? Well, I live in a land of metaphor and analogy. It's the way my brain functions. For me to understand a new concept or idea, I need to find something else to which I can relate this new thing. Otherwise, the new concept or idea is lost on me (just ask my family), or at the least I have to struggle mightily to grasp ahold of the new idea.

I have discovered that *most of us* do a better job of hanging on to new knowledge if we are given a meaningful metaphor or analogy as part of our learning process. So . . . Reality on a Bun, a concept by which I present "reality" (life) as an IT leader in small, easily digestible chunks (like a hamburger patty) on the "bun," (one "meal's" worth of information at a time). After all, no matter how motivated and eager we may be, there is only one way to eat a cow (should you desire to do that!) — and that's one bite at a time.

It is a bold assertion I make in the book's title, no? Twenty-five years' worth of lessons related to effective IT leadership — all in this little book? Well, there is no way I could possible distill everything I've learned in 25 years into a few pages. It's pretty clear that I have not seen everything, nor is there any way that I know it *all* about IT leadership. But I have seen many things, and I have had the chance to learn a few lessons. Do not consider my writings here to be "the answers"; instead, consider what I have written as another perspective, a chance to read and hear — and potentially learn from someone else's experiences.

In my 25+ years as an IT professional, I have seen little management, leadership, or effectiveness material devoted to the IT professional. Instead, it's as if we have to take the lowest common denominator approach to "normal" management training and adapt it to the world of IT. As *all* IT professionals know, IT is different. (And so are we! Just ask my wife.) Always has been, and always will be. My objective is to provide new insight and perspective related to the specifics of life as an IT leader. I have high hopes for my objective!

Let's set the stage. To do that, I like to think about a Saturday Night Live bit I saw years ago. The premise was this: After being out of college for 10 years or more, you were able to summarize all that you learned in college in five minutes. The joke continued with the "Five-Minute University" pitchman asking, "Want a Law Degree? Got a Minute?" The point is I have tried to take the most important things I have learned in 25 years and summarize them in these pages. I wish I would have been given this book when I was just starting out. What a difference it would have made.

I believe this book will have gold nuggets for anyone who works as an IT leader (from night operations shift supervisors to CIOs of Global 3000 companies), anyone who aspires to be an IT leader, or anyone who manages, works with, or wants to know more about how IT leaders "tick." As you read, rest assured I will try my best not to haul out all the obvious stuff you've already seen or can read in other publications. I will avoid talking about best practices of project management, zero-cost budgeting, Stephen Covey's seven habits, and other such things. Instead, I am going to keep the discussion centered around my own observations, assertions, and personal synthesis.

Not everything in this book will apply to you, nor is it intended to do so. Nor do I expect you to agree with everything in here. However, once you have finished reading, I do hope you find yourself saying, "Hmm ... I hadn't thought of that before." If you do, I will have been successful!

With that, let's get started.

Chapter 1: Dancing with the Bear
Leading Something Ugly

*P*ost dot-com, post Y2K, post client/server, and post open systems, we see that the binge on tech spending during the 80s and 90s has caused a hangover in the IT industry that will last for years. It's almost as if the historical (and hysterical) "just say yes" dynamics of IT investment have been replaced with (the equally hysterical) "just say no." Some might believe external forces such as a poor economy, global political instability, terrorism, and so forth are to blame for the slowdown in tech-related spending. But rather than blame factors beyond our control, we must pay attention to a more dramatic and systemic change that is evolving in the world of IT spending within our corporations and institutions. IT leaders of today must *really* justify our existence. This is a new dynamic for us, and it is confusing to many IT professionals.

Historically, business leaders have been willing to throw money at IT and just hope, because almost since its inception some 50 years ago, IT has held a special place within business investment. As such, IT spending has not been held to the same rigorous justification models as spending on other business-related investments. Why? Call it the novelty factor. For decades, IT developments held the promise of massive business benefit

— and in many cases actually delivered some. However, in too many cases, the promise wasn't manifested in real, measurable terms. Look at the dot-com mania as an example. How many companies wasted money, chasing something that didn't deliver any benefit to their organizations? Too many times in the past, business people simply followed the bouncing ball of technology and spent, spent, spent. That is, until the bill for dot-com came due. Enter the bear named ROI.

> *The dot-com bomb was the last straw related to "let's throw money at IT and hope" thinking. Forever more, business people won't just believe the promises of IT-related ROI without proof.*
>
> *Can you say "hello" to the bear named ROI?*

IT leaders will forever more compete for the same capital expenditure and operational budget dollars as our counterparts in manufacturing, logistics, engineering, administration, sales, and marketing. As such, IT leaders need to think and act like business leaders. But because to this point in our industry we've been more focused on innovating the technologies we use than we have been *applying* the technologies to deliver business results, many IT leaders are baffled by the "hows" of competing.

Too often in the past, IT leaders spent most of their education funds on classes related to the newest, latest technology. Little, if any, was spent on education related to solving business challenges. That philosophy is outdated, and if an IT leader continues operating with that point of view, he or she will find it dangerously career-limiting.

I'm reminded of a story from a situation with a client. I had the chance to speak at the annual meeting for the IT department of a Fortune 500 manufacturing company. I think my presentation was about career planning into the 21st century, or some other pithy title like that. Anyway, there was one caveat. The CEO of this company also was to address the IT department, and the only time he had available was right in the middle of my presentation. He was to speak for about 10 minutes. I said, "That's great! He's the CEO, and he's paying my bill. Perfect!"

Off I went with my presentation — describing the issues, etc., associated with career planning, blah, blah, blah. Then, just as I was making a point about understanding business needs and how important that is to IT career development, here came the CEO. I sat down, and he started talking. He gave an eloquent, thorough, and balanced presentation during his 10 minutes — describing the most significant business challenges facing the organization, new metrics the company was using to measure success, plans for the future, and so on. It was an excellent snapshot of the state of the business and its future needs.

He left, I stood back up, I paused. I looked at the IT department, and instead of resuming right where I had left off in my presentation, I asked the following, "Who took notes?" Pause. Long pause. No hands. It's amazing how about 200 people in the room instantly had to see whether there were any messages or pressing issues that might have appeared on their PDAs or cell phones. People stared at the ceiling, shifted in their seats, started biting their fingernails — anything but answer my question. Getting a sense the audience was feeling *very* uncomfortable, I decided to jump right into the middle of their discomfort (being a consultant does have its advantages!).

I then said (as if I were answering the question for them), "You mean we were supposed to pay attention?" Point made. The CEO had just given them the secret formula for their departmental (and thus individual) success. Solve the business problems, and we win. If we win, you win.

Granted, it's *hard* to deliver solutions that help businesses and organizations become more competitive and successful! We've got to dance with the bear now, and as we all know, bears are big, slow, tough to teach, and smelly, and they have the potential to rip us from limb to limb at any point in time. In other words, we used to be able to implement a new technology and hope for positive outcomes. Now, we have to prove the outcome before we start. *We must lead* because the market isn't helping to do that for us.

Why? Several reasons. Without some massive new shift in the human/machine interface, we've maxed out our abilities to deliver any significantly different "ways of life" through technology. Personal computers? Done. Connecting the world? On the way. Enterprise applications? Written. We still need to finish installing them, but they're written. So what's left? Virtual reality? Please. Wearable computers? Not a chance (my laptop is already joined to my body). PDA-based business applications? Maybe some.

We've pretty much maxed out our super-new, wildly different technology choices for a while. I'm sure there's something on somebody's drawing board somewhere that will start a new tech-based revolution, but it may be decades away. In the meantime, the bear is breathing down our necks — and we all know how disgusting bear breath is. It's time for us to turn inward and stop looking outwardly.

If you are serious about being an IT leader, it is imperative that you learn how to successfully deliver *real* business value using IT solutions. Take notes the next time your CEO speaks. Read a business magazine or two. Tear apart your company's balance sheet and look for real investment opportunities (e.g., reduce working capital, improve inventory turns, shorten lead time and cycle times), join the Chamber of Commerce in addition to the local WebSphere users group. Get steeped in biz-speak, not tech-speak. Now is the time for IT leaders to lead businesses toward better results by leveraging appropriate IT solutions. It's our mission, our obligation.

Teaching the bear to dance to your music isn't just necessary as an IT leader; it's also the best way to keep your job. This is the impetus for this book: Being an effective IT leader isn't optional any longer. It is required.

> *Delivering business value must be the number one goal of every IT leader. Continuing to put "tech-head" priorities ahead of business needs will prove to be amazingly career shortening.*

Chapter 2: Leadership 101
Real leadership is elusive

*L*ooking for leadership is a life-long quest for some. IT leadership comes in many different forms and flavors — from the night operations shift leader to the CIO. Before I jump in and describe just what makes IT leadership different from regular business leadership (it is!), let's take a few minutes to explore the notion of leadership altogether.

I believe all human beings are deeply, subconsciously, and passionately searching for leadership. However, leadership is an elusive quality that appears only when it is real. Like *The Velveteen Rabbit*, "realness" takes time, character, risk, objectivity, pain, trial, failure, and love. Real leadership is a rare, brilliant gem that surprises us when we are in its presence.

An excerpt from *The Velveteen Rabbit*, by Margery Williams:

> *"What is REAL?" asked the Rabbit one day, when they were lying side by side near the nursery fender, before Nana came to tidy the room. "Does it mean having things that buzz inside you and a stick-out handle?"*

> "Real isn't how you are made," said the Skin Horse. "It's a thing that happens to you. When a child loves you for a long, long time, not just to play with, but REALLY loves you, then you become Real."
>
> "Does it hurt?" asked the Rabbit.
>
> "Sometimes," said the Skin Horse, for he was always truthful. "When you are Real you don't mind being hurt."
>
> "Does it happen all at once, like being wound up," he asked, "or bit by bit?"
>
> "It doesn't happen all at once," said the Skin Horse. "You become. It takes a long time. That's why it doesn't happen often to people who break easily, or have sharp edges, or who have to be carefully kept. Generally, by the time you are Real, most of your hair has been loved off, and your eyes drop out and you get loose in your joints and very shabby. But these things don't matter at all, because once you are Real you can't be ugly, except to people who don't understand."

Unfortunately, because *real* leadership appears infrequently, our thirst goes unabated. We often substitute popularity, money, or a loud voice for leadership. You know what I mean: whoever is most popular with the boss, has the most money, or speaks the loudest tends to become the leader of the group. We confuse management, direction, or control with leadership — and as such, we expect our managers, directors, and controllers to lead. Many times, this is an unrealizable expectation.

We also confuse leadership with power. Power is something given, not exerted. In America, we let our government be in power because we've given them the power, not because they've taken it. Other countries may not follow this same approach at times, but given enough time, even the most "powerful" dictators and extremist "leaders" will eventually fall. All of them have, since the beginning of time.

Therefore, do not confuse leadership with the ability to be powerful over someone else. In fact, I look at it in the opposite way. True leaders are the best servants. Another point of distinction here: Do not confuse service with being subservient. These are two different things. Servant leaders look out for the needs of whomever they are serving and provide assisting service. Subservient persons give away their personal power to others and live life as a doormat. Remember, great leaders are great servants first.

Let's let that sink in for a second. Servant leadership. It seems strange to connect these words in this way. Servant leadership. *Living* those words — well, that's an entirely different story. One of the basic premises of this book is that IT leadership is unique in some ways. Let's take a look at some of the ways real IT leadership makes itself known within a business or organization:

Leadership 101 Stuff

- Real leaders never ask anyone to do something they wouldn't do, or haven't done, themselves.
  - o Don't ask someone to stay late and finish a project when you regularly and consistently leave the office early or at 5:02 p.m.
- Live the quote from Harry S. Truman: *"You can accomplish anything in life, provided that you do not mind who gets the credit."* I have this at the end of my e-mail signature, and I see it 20 to 30 times a day (sometimes more!). I need regular reminding about this. (It's my hero complex that gets in the way.)

- Get your hands dirty. Servant leaders, while not responsible for the actual "doing" of most work, are clearly hands-on in the eyes of their followers. If you only swoop in here and there to offer advice and to give directives, that's not leadership. That's trying to make yourself important.

- Have integrity. You must align your words and your actions. There is no other option here.

  o Don't ask your administrative assistant to lie about your whereabouts just because you do not want to take a call or hold a meeting; be accountable for your own schedule.

- Lavish praise and give attribution to others. Stay away from any self-congratulations. You'll have time to present your case when you meet with your boss (see the section Expectation Handling with Your Boss in Chapter 7).

- Great servant leaders do not seek the spotlight — they shun it.

Business-Focused IT Leadership

That is some basic stuff about servant leadership. I can hear some of you saying, "But that will never work in the context of IT. Most people do not 'get it' about IT stuff. How can I be a servant leader to them?" Here are some thoughts:

- Users are to be respected, not patronized or belittled — in public and in IT in "behind closed door" meetings as well.

- Technical knowledge, in and of itself, is basically useless. It's only the *application of the technical knowledge* to solve business problems that is important.

- Business competence among IT leaders is more important than technical knowledge (take off those propeller beanies!). Period.

- Real IT leaders explore the *value to the business* of emerging and evolving technology-related solutions. They do not waste time or resources exploring options that are simply fun and distracting to techie-types.

- When a non-IT person doesn't understand a term, some jargon, or other techie-talk stuff, and the concept or idea of the technology is valid to the business, the real IT leader becomes a teacher. The IT leader explains or demonstrates the technology-related solution in a way that the non-IT person understands it.

Internal IT Departmental IT Leadership

Now, what about IT leaders leading IT types? Take everything presented so far and amplify it. Remember, just as kids watch every move their parents make, looking for any chink in the armor (oh, it works every third time I go around Dad and ask Mom), a real IT leader leads his or her staff by example.

- IT types tend to value themselves based upon the currency and depth of their technical knowledge.

  o Fight for chances to offer training.

  o Don't simply defer to upper management when they ask you to cut training dollars. If you have to cut, then you have to cut — but fight for things your staff find important to them, and they'll fight for you in return.

- Be specific, balanced, and comprehensive when describing business issues at hand.

  o Help those whom you are leading to discover ways to solve business problems through their technical acumen.

- Make sure compensation is competitive.

- o When right, salaries should be about fifth or sixth on the list of job satisfiers. When wrong, salaries move to the number one dissatisfier.

- o If other departments offer stock options, comp-days, outings, and social event support, do that too!

- Make the tough decisions to ensure you have the right people on your team (see Chapter 6, Hiring, Assembling, and Leading Teams).

Leading as a Manager

Opportunities to show leadership within an IT department are nearly boundless. Showing real leadership at critical times with your staff is one of the most important chances to demonstrate your leadership and grow as a leader. Our industry has been shaken by the dot-bomb fallout and the hangover resulting from other under-value spending on IT by businesses. As a result, many of us have had to make difficult personnel-related decisions to reduce staff. How many of you reading have *not* had to lay someone off or have not been laid off yourself? Raise your hands if neither has been part of your life in the past. Anyone?

Other difficult times — particularly when we act as managers — present themselves on a regular basis. Employees need to be counseled or coached about poor behavior, unacceptable performance reviews, promotions not received, and so on. In each of these situations, it becomes extremely tempting to simply hide behind our managerial responsibilities and make hard business decisions.

Managers may not be responsible for company, overall departmental, or even workgroup leadership, but each manager has the chance to demonstrate leadership qualities. Here are some examples:

- Giving a negative review or presenting the need for corrective action on the part of an under-performing employee.

- o   A real leader will present the facts surrounding the situation, will describe specifically where and how the employee's actions have fallen short, and then will describe the course of action (and measurements) related to expected corrective measures. Specifics. No "just fix it" statements.
- o   At *no* time will any personal attack be allowed. You will discuss the issues and describe the behaviors, but you will not belittle or shame the person receiving the bad news.

- Telling a valued employee (potentially even a friend) that due to budgetary considerations, they're being laid off.
  - o   A real leader will be courageous, honest, and professional when having to lay off an employee.
  - o   Compassion and empathy are more important qualities during a layoff than HR "talking points." Don't run afoul of the law (or your corporate attorney), but you can lay off employees with concern for their well-being and their future.

I believe it's just the right thing to do — to treat others as I would like to be treated. If a more cynical view fits you better, keep in mind that our industry is a big small town (if you get my meaning). What goes around comes around. Who knows, you may find yourself interviewing for a job with someone you once laid off or to whom you gave some job-related direction. Make sure they're pleased to see you.

> *Great leaders are great servants first.*
> *Being a great servant means being a great listener.*
>
> *Great leaders do not have to be heard.*

Chapter 3: Analyzing the Industry
Hype Debunking, Reality Finding

*G*etting a handle on how to make IT-related decisions is a difficult, problem-prone undertaking. It is also one of the most important qualities of an effective IT leader. Successfully analyzing our industry is more difficult because IT is young (50 years is a short time in the span of humanity) and also because it's based on ongoing and regular innovation. Think about it. How many other professions work as hard as possible to make obsolete its foundation, its tools, and its methods?

Medicine? No way. We've been building our collective knowledge about chemistry, herbs, holistic cures, and so on since time began. Clearly, we use a lot of technology here, but it tends to build upon itself, not replace itself.

Law? Nope. Shelves literally creak under the weight of all the legal cases that have ever been filed. Experts spend their entire lives becoming adept at citing the vast amonts of information and precedents stored in legal libraries.

Accounting? Please. Innovations in the world of accounting usually lead to opportunities to provide testimony at Senate hearings.

Sports? Entertainment? Manufacturing? Finance? Insurance? Certainly there is a correlation between competitiveness and uses of technology in many industries (look at motor sports, for example), but to a large degree, it's the IT world that is leading the charge in innovation and change in these industries. We've innovated manufacturing technology using robotics and shrunk things to tinier and tinier sizes, but massive and pervasive changes in manufacturing technologies do not happen nearly as frequently and regularly when compared to changes in *IT-related technologies.*

In the IT department, we literally are faced with the potential of completely revamping and redoing our technology architectures (e.g., operating systems, servers, networks, security, databases), development tools (e.g., programming languages, scripting languages, control languages, developer environments), and presentation tools (e.g., browsers, PC operating systems, PDAs, phones) about every 10 years. However (and this is a big however), simply chasing changes in technology because the technology has changed is nearly never a wise strategy for most businesses.

What about the research organizations out there such as Gartner, IDC, and Forrester? Aren't these companies in business to help sort out options related to technology purchases? Well . . . um . . . er. That's what their marketing types would like you to believe.

> *My experience tells me that research companies can be just as clueless as the rest of us. After all, how many of them accurately told the story about the dot-com build-up and blow-out?*
> **None of them, that's how many.**

Certainly research coming from these companies and others does have some value — but don't believe it at face value. We need to ensure our common sense and "gut checks" get just as much credence as the research organizations' data and pretty PowerPoint presentations. One of my favorite moments as a pain-in-the-neck consultant came when I got the chance to hear from one company's "grand pooh-bah" analyst, who was attempting to show data about operating system penetration in the market. He was proudly showing their latest chart of assertions about which operating systems would be in use in the next five years.

Unfortunately for him, he did not know I had come "loaded" for him. I had the same chart, from the same company, but it was five years old. I hauled out the chart and showed it to him. I asked, "Did your company prepare this chart?" Pause. "Yes." "Is it an accurate reflection of today's reality?" I asked. Long pause. "No." "Well, then, why should I believe the chart you just showed us?" Oh, if there had been a hole to crawl into, or better yet to send me into, he would have done it. Believe me, he never recovered — and found the earliest excuse to leave the room.

Again, the research does have value, but make sure you put your own "sniff test" to work. If you have other research against which to correlate or corroborate, do it! I can't tell you how many people simply include Gartner, Forrester, AMR, or IDC charts or graphs in their presentations without thinking about them at all. With that as a backdrop, here are two simple "lessons" I learned about evaluating the IT industry trends and directions:

- Beware the fad, beware the novelty. I remember back in November of 1980 — our first child, Amanda, was just a newborn — Debi and I bought a microwave oven. It was expensive and revolutionary. And like most people back then, we tried making everything in it (Debi loves cookbooks, and the new microwave came with a whole series). We tried cakes, turkeys — all sorts of things. Unfortunately, turkey skin coming out of a microwave is just a little too similar to human skin to make me comfortable, and cakes — well, they were a bit like beige puddles. Alas, the novelty of the microwave wore off, and now, like most people, we use ours for popcorn, hot water, and reheating leftovers. We can't imagine *not* having a microwave, but the originally intended uses for it were unrealized in reality.

- Vendors, authors, and consultants always have something to gain with revolutions in technology. As such, check to see whether the person advocating the technology has something to gain if you end up purchasing the technology. If someone is selling you a new technology, and they have a month-end or quarter-end deal for you, tell them you are going to wait.

Simply put, technologies come, and some may stay, but the vast majority go. For evidence to support this assertion, let's look at some of the hottest technologies from the past and see where they are today.

CASE (Computer Assisted Software Engineering)

- I remember large technology vendors claiming that CASE would permanently change the way software would be written. As such, an analyst would "map" the business processes and workflow into a program generator, and out would pop the software. Additionally, since the business rules and workflow were by themselves platform neutral, the code generator could be tweaked to create software for virtually any operating system or database. A darn cool idea — particularly for businesses looking for high quality in software, lower costs to produce it, and more flexibility in making changes to it!

- However, CASE failed, and failed badly. Why? Not because it was the wrong answer — but because human nature caused it to fail. Technologists are humans after all (regardless of what others say!), and we have our share of fears and insecurities. Once the development community *really* understood that CASE would make programmers redundant (or at least that was the perception), developers sabotaged CASE. No, we didn't move to overt operations, mobilizing ourselves to actively disrupt CASE's progress; we just refused to support it. As such, only a few companies really embraced the technology, and CASE died by being ignored.

Open Systems

- Quiz!!! What is POSIX, and why was it vital to technology-related decision-making in the late 1980s and early 1990s? Tick, tick, tick. I am always amazed at how few hands go up when I ask this question of attendees at one of my IT-related workshops.

- What is POSIX? The IEEE (Institute of Electrical and Electronics Engineers) defines POSIX as Portable Operating System Interface (POSIX). Here's some language that may help from the PASC (Portable Applications Standards Committee of the IEEE):

    The original, trial-use standard published in 1986 was actually called IEEE-IX (IEEE's version of UNIX). However, this was rapidly changed to POSIX in time for the second printing (also in 1986).

    The standard is heavily influenced by UNIX®, and in the latest revision now merges with The Open Group's Base Specifications, which constitute the core of the Single UNIX Specification. In the mid-eighties, there was a plethora of UNIX operating systems, most of which had names ending in X (e.g., HPUX, AIX, PNX, Xenix), and that certainly influenced the naming decision.

The following quotation appears in the Introduction to POSIX.1:

> *"The name POSIX was suggested by Richard Stallman. It is expected to be pronounced pahz-icks as in positive, not poh-six, or other variations. The pronunciation has been published in an attempt to promulgate a standardized way of referring to a standard operating system interface."* (Editorial comment: Interesting need to publish standard pronunciation rules for a standard. RST)

- Okay — again, what is POSIX? You've just read the IEEE definition, but does that help you understand why it was so vital in the late 80s? No. Back then, POSIX was used to define open systems — a concept that vendors tried to make end users fall in love with so that all applications could be deemed standardized, thus ensuring interoperability and consistency. The thought was that open systems would create more "consumer benefits" for end users as they were able to pick and choose from open solutions.

- While the benefits of open systems have been realized to some degree within the world of software development, the assertion that openness would translate into consumer benefit fell flat on its face. Chief among the reasons openness (as envisioned) failed has to do with the fact that vendors couldn't compete in a purely commodity-based market. As such, many of the vendors who jumped on the open-systems bandwagon in a big way are no longer in business or were purchased by others. Remember Sequent? Digital Equipment Corporation? Poof.

Client/Server

- Now, this idea actually had lots of vendors, authors, and consultants salivating over the possibilities. Let's let each user (or department) pick his or her PC, then we'll hook up these thousands of dissimilar PCs, located all over the world, to a growing network of specialized servers, all running different operating systems, databases, security monitors, and so on. OOOO-eee! What fun for propeller heads! In fact, client/server was one of the greatest chances for techie types to rule the world.

• However, client/server can also be placed on the list of technologies whose 15 minutes of fame is over. Businesses finally came to their senses and realized that heterogeneity in technology, while maybe good for the individual's psyche, is *terrible* for the bottom line. As such, companies are looking to standardize their technology infrastructures to eliminate differences. Homogeneity in technology is now the right answer, and browser-based user interfaces are replacing fat PC-based applications as quickly as possible.

Beware the Pendulum

The tough thing about technology-related pendulums is they swing both ways. On one hand, you get irrational glee, and on the other, irrational glum. Glee, glum, glee, glum — back and forth. Public opinion moves back and forth with the stock market or with other irrational market forces (yes, the stock market defies rational definition most of the time).

Whenever large groups of people start to believe something — without questioning the downside — a psychological process called "group think" emerges. General George Patton once said, "If everyone's thinking the same way, then someone's not thinking." He had an excellent definition of group think. Hans Christian Andersen's *The Emperor's New Clothes* is a story about group think (although I am not sure Hans attended Psychology 101!), and so is the story about the dot-com build-up and subsequent blow-out.

> *Once upon a time there lived a vain Emperor whose only worry in life was to dress in elegant clothes. He changed clothes almost every hour and loved to show them off to his people.*
>
> *Word of the Emperor's refined habits spread over his kingdom and beyond. Two scoundrels who had heard of the Emperor's*
>
> *vanity decided to take advantage of it. They introduced themselves at the gates of the palace with a scheme in mind.*
>
> *"We are two very good tailors and after many years of research we have invented an extraordinary method to weave a cloth so light and fine that it looks invisible. As a matter of fact it is invisible to anyone who is too stupid and incompetent to appreciate its quality."*

Sound familiar? How many of you *really* believed that the e-economy was going to forever change the habits and culture of humans substantively and sustainably? Really. On the other hand, does anyone out there sense that group think was going on during the massive e-business–fueled run-up of the NASDAQ during 1999?

At one point during 2000 (March 10, to be specific), the NASDAQ exceeded 5100, Cicso's market cap was about $555 billion (along with a P/E ratio approaching 200), making it the most highly valued company in the world, and the "on paper millionaires' club" added nearly four million more members during the 1997-2000 time frame.

Excitement, giddy prognostications, self-congratulations, and general overall cultural insanity took over. Then, the bubble burst. Amazing to me, many people were surprised that the gravy train derailed, but a sense of "where's the beef" returned to investment-based decision-making. Without profits, there would be no more investment. Poof.

The liquid capital markets dried up faster than a spilled water bottle in the Sahara Desert. People remained surprised and shocked that the "recovery" wasn't immediate and complete.

In the 1997-1999 time frame, Internet-based technology investment was a no-brainer. No one got fired for recommending multi-million dollar Web-based initiatives; the lemmings were literally jumping over the browser-enabled cliff into the abyss of e-business. Expectations were rampant, and then, reality bites.

So, the pendulum has swung the other way. Along with anything looking like white powder, business leaders are unreasonably paranoid about spending on technology-based initiatives today. This is absurd — and extremely shortsighted. Much about business success remains consistent, which is good news for us in the IT profession (particularly those building their careers around e-business technologies and solutions).

Let's look at success factors needed in business — today, last year, 20 years ago, 10,000 years ago, and 10,000 years from now. Business leaders need courage, vision, and capital. That's been true forever and will be true forever.

What About the Next New Thing?

Remember that authors, vendors, and consultants (I have to be careful here; I represent all three!) will continue to try and create the next "new" thing for IT. It's their job — that's what they get paid to do! However, we as consumers do not have to jump every time something new comes out. As an industry, for example, we're currently evaluating the potential for wireless network delivery to PDA-type devices.

However, remember that while cellular phones are very popular, they didn't revolutionize human communication. I once read a story about a man and a woman in the 1860s who conducted a telegraph love affair. While it may take a really long time to say "What are you wearing?" in dots and dashes ;-), they did it. I'm sure there have been smoke-signal and jungle-drum love affairs as well. Thus, cellular phones have just made human communication more convenient; they didn't revolutionize it. I personally do not see how attaching a camera, or being able to play a Karate game, on my cellular phone makes anything better. It's that novelty thing again.

> *Novelty is great for kids' toys and April Fool's Day gags, but it has no place in the world of business. IT leaders look for business value, not "gee-whiz."*

Furthermore, these same marketing types are pushing Web services at us — telling us how important it is to be able to link applications on any system to applications on any other system — all using standard Internet protocols. However, what's missing in today's world is the ROI model that will pay for Web services. Unfortunately, there is not one. Maybe I have become too cynical and skeptical, but I am just not all that impressed with most new technologies. I wait until I see real business needs, and then I go looking for potential technology solutions. That's proven to be a good strategy for my clients and my employers.

Would you like to create some sustainable, long-term wealth for yourself and your company? Yes? Then it's time for IT professionals like us to take the best tools, the best technologies, and the best business processes and aid our companies in their pursuit of competitive advantage in today's economy.

If your company took a wrong turn a while back, instead of wagging your finger at your executives, show them the path to use technology to their advantage. (Don't fall into the trap of saying to someone "I told you so." No matter the personal glee you might gain as a result, it's still bad manners to use those words.) There's never been a better time to move forward boldly! Oh, and beware the pendulum. It will swing back the other direction — probably sooner rather than later.

Chapter 4: Creativ-IT-y Breeds Success
Innovation, Creativity, Insight

So ... life in IT is forever different, and the go-go days of IT spending are behind us. IT leaders are now in competition for corporate investment dollars — just like all the other departments in business. With the switch from "just say yes" to "just say no," IT doesn't seem to hold the same promise for business benefit as it did 10 years ago. The landscape is charred, the prospects are dim, and the future looks bleak for IT spending and IT careers. Right? Many IT leaders look at it that way — but I don't.

Instead, I choose to look through a different lens, and I choose to expect different outcomes. Just as the lodgepole pine has evolved to regenerate after a fire (its serotinous cones open and drop their seeds only after being exposed to great heat), I believe IT is poised to come back from the post-90s/early-00s slump. Prudent investments in IT still have the promise to deliver significant business ROI. Many businesses still have dis-integrated, outdated, and redundant processes in place, so the right investment in IT can bring improved business productivity and profitability.

As I discussed in the previous chapter, I believe it's pointless to hope that the "next new, new thing" technology will be enough to revive spending on technology. Thus, rushing to the door of Web services or wireless applications to pay homage and hoping for business acceleration through tech demand will gain you nothing. Our history of just letting the technology speak for itself is also outdated. IT is quickly becoming commoditized as businesses reject "gee-whiz" stuff and the demand increases to differentiate IT's value in business. We need more than just more tech-head mumbo-jumbo.

As IT leaders look to stand apart from the other competing parts of the business, a new dynamic is evolving. Consumers in general always respond favorably to new approaches, new overtures, and new perspectives. Real people have always differentiated vendors on the vendor's ability to be creative — and memorable. It's a new day for IT leaders for getting our messages heard and understood within our businesses. Today, an IT leader must understand and deliver against the expectation of creativity and innovation. However, this is in direct opposition to what we've believed for decades.

> *Innovation, not process or methods.*
> *Creativity, not persuasive techniques.*
> *Insight, not research.*
>
> *These will be higher priorities in the future in IT-related activities.*

Oh, I can hear the purists out there cringing already. "What do you mean, insight is more important than research? And, how can you ensure success if you look toward innovation instead of process? Our 'best practices' are what we use to make sure we meet expectations." (Does this sound to you like a generic, "big firm" consultant? It does to me.) Here's one of the dirty little secrets from the world of big firm consulting: Best practices and methodologies are designed more to assist the consulting firm in collecting their fees than to assist their clients in getting the best possible results. No consultant really wants you to know that, but it's true.

How many times have you heard the term "best practices" in the past month? Hundreds? Just hearing that term causes me to roll my eyes. Geez. Best practices — according to whom?

As a result of our homogeneous approach to delivering IT services, our industry has become very "me too." This dynamic shows up in the world of telecommunications, where all the big players (AT&T, Verizon, Qwest) seem to be struggling to find competitive differentiation.

The problem is, after a decade or two of using consultants from the big firms — where the methods are pretty much the same, the processes seem very similar, and the consultants are indoctrinated using approaches that mirror each other — the telecom firms seem to have exactly the same problems. Each of these telecom companies has bloated systems, overly complex business rules, poor responsiveness, and shrinking differentiation. Not surprisingly, as many IT leaders have lost their own edge, they have also lost their ability to help their customers, clients, and stakeholders stand out above the crowd.

This is not always true, particularly in the world of consumer-packaged goods. Before a company such as Proctor & Gamble or Warner-Lambert actually brings a new product to market, they've invested millions in ideas that proved not to work. They most likely had about 3,000 ideas, of which only about four to five then received the go-ahead for market testing. Only about one to two of the original 3,000 ideas actually end up on the shelves at your local grocery store. It's an expensive process — but one that's necessary to meet a demanding public's expectation.

Consumers are consumers, whether we're buying laundry soap or Web services, and we're more and more demanding all the time. As such, let's examine the issue of creativity at work. Inventiveness and innovation are not just "nice to haves" any longer. Research is starting to show the economic future of entire cities, regions, and industries may rely on "creative competitiveness." Richard Florida, Ph.D., author of the book *The Rise of the Creative Class,* is a researcher and professor at Carnegie Mellon University.

"Cities that want to grow had better be creative," Florida says. Further, he argues that "the cities that appeal to the creative vanguard will prosper in an economy driven by inventiveness."

While Florida's comments above relate primarily to cities and geographic regions, he also argues that his research applies to industries, companies, and other institutions. In comments more specific to IT, Florida suggests, "There's a deeper unifying theme, too. What growing numbers of people seek in their work is basically this: They want to be creative. Creativity is a word not often associated with IT workers.

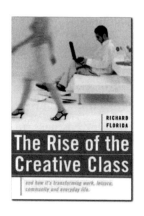

"But look more closely at the examples. The young software developer with tattoos and headphones is literally wearing art and music, and he's obviously being creative at work when he writes new code. Raising children demands nonstop creativity of the working mother; she's being creative when she looks for new ways to do her job — which, incidentally, may turn out to be better than the standard 'company way.'"

> *The dirty little secret of relying upon best practices and methods isn't designed to assist consumers of IT solutions in getting the best possible results.*
>
> *Instead, as is endemic in our Western culture, we are rewarded for finding the first right answer, not the best right answer. Best practices and methods often represent the first right answer.*
>
> *Hiding behind best practices and methods isn't leading. It's hiding.*

Creativity. Something we can immediately identify when we see it (like a really good Super Bowl commercial), but for many of us, it seems to be difficult to make it come from our own heads. Is creativity something that only a select few, genetically lucky individuals possess? Certainly, like anything else, some people are more inclined toward creative thinking than others. However, also like anything else, each of us can learn more about the process of creativity.

The Creative Process

Some of you may be blessed with the ability to just be creative and have it actually work. I've been teaching creativity to kids, school groups, and business people for the better part of two decades, and through this experience, I've learned a few things. First, everyone can be creative (not just those to whom it comes more naturally)! It's true. However, the vast majority of us benefit greatly by following some basic steps and learning a bit about the process of being creative. Second, the more you practice at being creative, the better you become at it. Even the most grizzled and hardened nonbelievers can become better at being creative. Believe it.

Learning and practicing creativity requires a few basic things: the right climate, time to allow the process to unfold, following the "rules" of creativity, and a chance to actually use some the of the creative outcomes in real-life situations.

Creating a Climate for Creativity

Make sure you're able to fulfill the following requirements for your team members:

- **Challenge and involvement:** Team members are involved in operations, long-term goals, and in sharing a common vision. You can't expect the highest level of creativity if you let your team members play only bit parts in the process. They must be engaged and involved.

- **Physical interaction:** Team members have the ability to physically interact with each other. Virtual creativity doesn't work very well for most people. Home offices can be the creative process killer in many situations.

- **Freedom:** Team members have the opportunity for independence in their behavior, their dress, their attitudes, and their workspace.

- **Trust and openness:** Team members feel there is emotional safety in their relationship with each other and the leaders involved in the process.

- **Idea time:** Team members have time set aside for the exploration, identification, and elaboration of new ideas. Creativity doesn't follow a Day-Timer or PDA-based schedule.

- **Playfulness and humor:** The leader provides a setting for spontaneity and comfort or ease of behavior.

- **Conflict:** Team members enjoy the absence of personal and emotional tensions, fighting, aggression, and hostile behavior. Leave the politics at the door.

- **Idea support:** New ideas are treated with interest and respect.

- **Discussions:** Team members feel comfortable encountering and disputing differences of viewpoints, ideas, experiences, and knowledge.

- **Risk-taking:** Team members feel there is openness for new and creative ideas.

Does the list above describe the climate you have with your team members, your peers, your managers, and your stakeholders? Or, on the other hand, do you normally do the "historical techie thing" and tell those around you only what they want to hear, or only try to sell them things you know they want to buy? Some common wisdom goes like this: "If you always do what you've always done, you'll always get what you've always got." Without constant permission to explore new and innovative things, relationships become stale — and effectiveness suffers. Indeed, no methodology or PMO (Program Management Office) approach I've ever seen puts high value on regular and repeated innovation during the project delivery.

Remember the dirty little secret? Simply
relying upon best practices and methods will
probably mean your consultants will be paid
(which is a good thing if you're a consultant!),
but it doesn't ensure your organization will
have a leading solution. As the chart to the
right indicates, a high level of "efficient
differentiation" is needed to be a leader in
your market or industry.

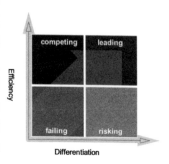

We'll talk more about efficiency in Chapter 10 (Measuring Your
Effectiveness). This chapter is all about differentiation (being innovative,
memorable, and unique), and creativity is a major component in achieving
a unique position in the market.

Creativity Fosters Authentic Relationships

Establishing and fostering a climate of creativity leads directly toward more
effective and market-leading solutions for my clients and for the businesses
for whom I work. Why? Partly, I attribute it to the need for openness and
vulnerability in the creative process. Simply by becoming real with my
clients (and they with me), we operate from a much more authentic place.
Then, as trust builds as we go through the creative process, we find ourselves
needing each other's perspectives as we examine potential options. We truly
become team members through this process.

Contrary to what many in the IT professional services business may hold
near and dear, I think being an authentic team member with my clients is
far better than "owning" the relationship any day. I've also found this to
be true within the context of an IT department. Too often, IT is separated
from the business anyway (there are many kinds of separations — cultural,
physical, attitudinal), and sadly, it is rare to actually witness an authentic

relationship between a business and its IT department. Break down some of the barriers! Create a climate for creativity — work together to play, to generate ideas, to take risks, to trust each other, and before you know it, you'll start to build an entirely different kind of relationship.

Thus, my experience tells me that establishing a climate for creativity fosters market differentiation, and it is also an excellent tool for building stronger relationships. Unfortunately, as a profession, we tend to be stuck in our heads — always looking for the logical, rational answer. Too many of us also believe that process, methods, and best practices are all that's needed to ensure success. I don't believe that's true.

IT leaders need to embrace creativity as a competitive tool — not just for the business overall, but for IT-related activities as well. If you are from the old school, I give you this caution: Beware the rising creative vanguard in the world of IT, those who are taking risks and assisting IT consumers in finding new, innovative solutions. These individuals are showing the way to deliver business results through IT investment.

To learn more about putting the creative process into action, I recommend many games, processes, and activities. For some ideas, I suggest you check out these books:

> Spolin, Viola. *Improvisation for the Theatre, 3rd Edition*. Northwestern University Press, 1999. ISBN: 081014008X.
> Thorpe, Scott. *How to Think Like Einstein*. Sourcebooks Trade, 2000. ISBN: 1570715858.
> Wise, Nina. *A Big New Free Happy Unusual Life*. Broadway Books, 2002. ISBN: 0767910079.

In the next chapter, you can begin to see where a creative approach can help with the marketing of your department — and the services you provide.

Chapter 5: Your IT Departmental Brand
Awareness, Understanding, Preference

We have become a marketing-driven society. In fact, some estimates suggest each of us is bombarded with thousands of marketing "impressions" each day (brand names, logos, jingles, blah, blah, blah). Having been part of a marketing organization in the past, I learned that the manipulation we feel may be there *is* really there. I took a class in college called Mass Media, in which we tore apart advertising and marketing messages to get to the hidden agenda. "Just what are they trying to make me feel" was our homework.

Even though I took that class some 20 years ago, I still can't watch commercials without tearing them apart. As such, never invite me over to watch the Super Bowl. I am no fun because I can't just enjoy the advertising; I have to ruin everyone's time by analyzing the messages! What does this have to do with an IT leader? Simply this: IT leaders, like any other business leaders competing for mindshare and budgets, need to understand the ins and outs of marketing messages and brand management strategies.

The sum total of marketing-related messages, together with actual experiences with a product or service, leads to the creation of a brand experience. What comes to mind when I say "Lexus"? Do you think about their message, "The relentless pursuit of perfection"?

Do you think about wanting a Lexus — because they are beautiful vehicles, with outstanding features, quality, and resale value? I believe most of you would answer yes to at least one of those questions. Some of you do not feel that way about Lexus, but most of you do!

 How about if I said "Enron" instead of "Lexus"? What feelings come to mind now?

Without really stating it, your IT department (or consulting business, or whatever) has a brand image in the minds of your consumers. I hear frequently from IT leaders, "Should my IT department have a brand?" That's an interesting question, but it's irrelevant. Even without pursuing a brand management strategy for your group, your IT department has a "perception," and too often the perception (okay, sort of like a brand) is not always positive. As a result, negatively perceived IT departments never seem to get enough respect and funding.

In the hundreds of IT departments I have studied, a poor IT departmental brand almost always translates into frustration, feelings of being taken for granted, not feeling appreciated, and generally poor relationships between the IT department and the business. This chapter is all about helping you if your departmental brand suffers due to poor PR or the lack of a good marketing approach. However, if your department has a history of poor results, nothing in a marketing strategy (or the words in this chapter) will overcome that. As such, focusing on delivery (see Chapters 9 and 10 on leading projects and measuring your effectiveness) needs to precede any marketing-related activities. Why don't more businesses understand that?

Get the product right first, then capitalize on the great product through a great brand strategy.

I was not a marketing major in college, nor have I spent years working in the marketing field. I am sure the marketing purists out there will cringe as they read the following few pages, but what I am about to share has worked in my experience of helping hundreds of IT departments sort through their options and choices related to creating and improving their IT brand. So there. ;-) If you support me this far, let's take a look at brand management for IT leaders — and the impact of having a positive perception (brand) within your market.

Looking for Desired Results

To be most effective, the process of managing your IT brand needs to have some outcome against which to measure success. (Duh. This is true for the entire human experience; we need measurable goals against which to hold ourselves accountable. See Chapter 10 about measuring your effectiveness.) Measurable goals need to be specific; simply stating "We want better customer service" doesn't cut it. Instead, it makes more sense to gear your brand strategy around helping your business (or clients) be more effective. Improving the image of your department is a valid activity, but without using that image improvement to support the business is a waste of time and resources. Look for ways your improved image will streamline the business, improve ROI, or optimize activities — and make that the cornerstone of your brand strategy.

> *If you are concerned about losing your job or being outsourced because the executives in your company do not have a positive impression of your IT departmental brand, work to change it.*

Give the CEO the chance to say, "Because I understand the offerings of our internal IT department, and prefer their approach to solving our business problems, there is no way in the world I would ever consider abdicating my IT function to an outsourced provider. Give me a break!"

Marketing Basics

I remember my Mass Media class once again. Our teacher made the following (really obvious) point: "All advertising is inherently deceptive." Duh again. Who believes that Britney Spears really gets that excited over a caramel-colored, carbonated, cola-flavored beverage? Don't confuse marketing with advertising. Advertising can be part of a marketing plan, but it's not essential. In fact, I do not advocate advertising as an IT departmental brand strategy. It should not be necessary.

That said, if we look at a marketing program for your IT brand (with a tip of my hat to Glen Metelmann, one of my early teachers in the world of marketing), the following pages describe the three basics any marketing program should attempt to achieve: Awareness, understanding, and preference.

Awareness

This is the easy one of the three. Awareness is the process of making your customers or potential customers aware of your existence. I believe all IT departments have some level of awareness within their businesses; if for no other reason, Y2K projects brought the spotlight to IT departments around the world. However, even with awareness, you may not have the right kind of awareness. I know a CIO who gave his heart and soul for his business for more than 18 years, delivering exceptional business results, and then one day got himself sideways with the CEO of the family business for dropping the ball on a totally insignificant-to-the-business project — but one that was very important to the CEO himself. The CIO feared for his job because the

CEO's awareness of the IT department's performance was severely clouded by a single project. This is the kind of awareness that nobody wants.

> The consumers of your IT-related services have to be aware of what you can do. If you just expect them to know without telling them, then you probably still think Santa Claus actually knows who is naughty and who is nice.

Awareness is the sum total of impressions a consumer has with the product or service — and too often in the case of IT department product and service, it's the "what have you done for me lately" situation that seems to be most pervasive. Going back to the fact that bad performance can't be overcome with good marketing, if you've just delivered something that is truly bad, it's better to admit it — and to work hard to change it. Make a covenant never to do it again (write on the board one thousand times: I will never put anything into production without full regression testing. I will never put anything into production without full regression testing.). All too often, small or insignificant problems — in the absence of otherwise positive awareness — are amplified beyond reasonable levels.

What can you do to improve the awareness of your IT brand? Read the book *Moments of Truth* by Jan Carlsson. He was the CEO of SAS Airlines, and upon taking the reins, he found himself with one of the worst-perceived brands in the airline business. He set out to change that by reminding his staff that every time someone comes across the SAS organization, it is a "moment of truth." Think about it: Every memo, every phone message, every e-mail, every newsletter, every phone call, every advertisement — every time anyone sees, hears, or touches your IT department, they have a chance to form an impression, which then leads to their perceived awareness of your organization. Read the book, and take its message to heart. It's great.

Understanding

Okay, now it gets more complicated. If we go back to what it means to be a servant IT leader — particularly to users and non-IT types who do not "get it" related to IT stuff — you'll remember I indicated that real IT leaders become teachers and help their students understand. Creating understanding about your IT department involves being specific and honest about your "product." You need to share details about costs, time frames, skill set strengths and weaknesses, methodologies, and so on.

Providing clear understanding of what your IT department can and can't do means being clear in your "stands" as a group. In other words, many departments choose to limit the variety of architectural components of their IT infrastructure. Keeping a lid on the proliferation of operating systems, databases, network management, programming languages, and so on is not only good for the bottom line (see Chapter 3, Analyzing the Industry), but also good as a building block in an IT departmental brand strategy.

> *Nobody believes that any group can do it all when it comes to IT services. Beware the tendency to oversell your own, or your group's, abilities as you look to justify your existence. In the long run, overstating things will cause you more harm than good.*

Again, understanding means teaching, and teaching means reaching students where they are, not where the teacher is. Take the time to develop tutorial programs (some groups do brown bag lunches where esoteric things such as Business Intelligence or Web services or Active Security Monitoring are topics for business people), and always explain. Always explain. Always explain. Disney does a good job here. When you ask *anyone* at one of their theme parks for directions to the rest rooms, he or she (from a janitor to

Michael Eisner himself) will also ask you if there is anything else he or she can do to help. Try asking for directions at Disneyland — and then stop the person before they ask you if you need something else. It is difficult. Disney employees are conditioned to go the extra step with their guests.

Preference

Every time I hear this word, it reminds me of a hair-coloring product sold by a company called L'Oréal. I bet you can hear the woman's voice as she says, "Preference, by L'Oréal. Because I'm worth it." There is a subtle but powerful message in that commercial. L'Oréal products cost more than their competitors, but to consumers who listen to the advertising message, they'll get the impression that they have "permission" to spend more, because they're worth it. Preferences are choices, made by individuals, and often these individuals need to be given permission to choose.

Certainly, a large part of the preference shown by a potential consumer has much to do with the quality, price, and overall experience with the product itself. However, when helping your executives get to "preference" with your approach to delivering IT services and products, remember to not simply rest on your laurels and the quality of your results to date. Make sure you are constantly reminding your customers that they have permission to choose your approach.

> *Getting your consumers to prefer your approach to IT services is a combination of messages and results. If your group can't deliver the goods, it doesn't matter how good your message is. Real preference takes time to build and, when manifested, is nearly bullet-proof.*

Brand Experience Journey

Finally, here's a chart that depicts a brand experience journey in the world of cars. In fact, this chart comes from the work done on the Audi America online site — some excellent work done by great people who worked for a professional services company that no longer exists. If you follow the chart, you'll see it's a 360-degree view — from initial awareness, to engagement and consideration (understanding), to purchase and ownership (preference), to disposal and reengagement.

This cycle happens with IT departments, too. It's just that we do not spend the necessary time and attention needed to understand this dynamic and to capitalize upon it. Like it or not, we are a marketing-driven society, and those who understand it, and ethically use marketing strategies, have advantages in overall effectiveness.

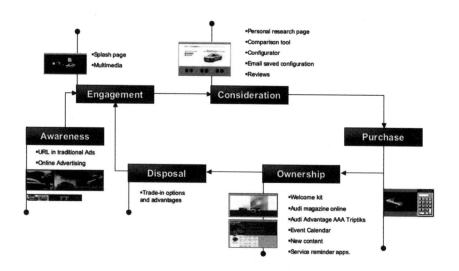

Chapter 6:
Hiring, Assembling, and Leading Teams
Great teams are no accident

*S*urrounding yourself with the right mix of talent and personalities is a critical early step in outfitting yourself for success. If you have the chance to build the teams with which you work, that's great! However, in my experience, most IT leaders inherit some if not most members of their teams. It is unlikely you will have the chance to hire all the members of your staff from scratch. I am fortunate to have done it once, but I had to start my own business to do it! In all other situations, I came into a department or organization that already had staff in place.

In addition, you may find yourself leading teams where you have no direct control over the team makeup. If you are the CIO or VP of IT, you most likely participate as the leader of a committee designed to prioritize and fund IT-related projects. Often called steering committees, these groups are composed of senior management coming from various departments and key stakeholders. You may also play a leadership role in various operations or policy-setting groups or committees. As such, you will find yourself leading teams you didn't assemble and in which you have little or no direct management responsibility.

This chapter takes a look at the three major activities related to teams: hiring, assembling, and leading. We'll examine my tried and true three rules of hiring, some key points related to assembling teams, and then various aspects of leading teams, including information about group dynamics, types of groups, and key roles played by various team members.

> *Few activities are more important to an effective leader than the ability to hire well, assemble great teams, and lead teams as they deliver against business expectations. As a leader, you will be measured more frequently by the success of the teams you lead, not by the efforts of your own hands.*

Hiring

Over the years, I have hired more than 2,000 people at various times and places. Just imagine the number of resumes I have read and the interviews I have conducted so I could hire that number of people. During all that time, I have developed a few tried and true rules about hiring.

I am not going to bore you with the details associated with normal HR-related activities. Yes, you've got to check references. Yes, background checks are becoming a requirement in hiring (e.g., criminal records, blood tests). I am going to assume you or your organization does an effective job in the administration and process of getting someone hired and in the door. What I would like to focus on is hiring the "right person" for your team.

I have three rules of hiring that I have developed — and trust.

Rule One: *Hire exceptional people.*

In other words, I hire people who are excellent at something. Scuba diving, piano playing, mountain climbing, singing, coaching baseball — I don't care, really. I just want to be around people who have dedicated themselves to excelling at some activity in their lives. Exceptional people understand the value of commitment, hard work, and personal accountability. To be truly excellent at something requires you to trade off between choices; it requires your diligence and effort. Look for excellent qualities in candidates.

Rule Two: *You must be better at what you do than I am at what you do.*

This rule may seem like a strange objective for a leader; after all, aren't leaders supposed to be the "experts"? I guess I have an alternative perspective on this. I do not ever want to feel as though I have to do someone else's job for them. I barely have time to do my own job! Additionally, one of the greatest (if not *the* greatest) human needs is one of acceptance and belonging. If a leader is always trying to do someone else's job, it invalidates the other person's need to belong. I know where my limitations are, so why would I hire people who are more limited than I am? That just doesn't make sense. Instead, if I hire people who do their job better than I could do their job, the overall team quality will increase exponentially. It becomes a situation where 1+1=3, 2+2=5, and so on.

Rule Three: *No whining.*

This might be the most important rule of all. Maybe it's because my wife and I are raising four kids, but I get more whining than I need in the rest of my life. I just do not have time for complaining, positioning, politicking, and useless noise coming from people in my work life. After all, aren't professionals supposed to be adults — able to resolve wounds of the past and take responsibility for their own lives? Oh, sorry. I digressed into a dreamland for a second.

Unfortunately, I have seen unkind correlations between someone's educational background, years of experience, training, or intelligence, and their "whiny-ness." Too often, the more educated someone is, the better the school they come from, and the more impressive their resume, the more they whine. Prima donnas, stay away from me and my department. I need everyone to grasp an oar and pull hard with me. I would much rather have a strong, team-oriented person with great potential than prima donnas who believe they're the source of all that's good and right.

I've hired some incredibly bright and educated staff members whom I couldn't stand. I let their pedigrees obliterate my three rules as I looked for the right person to hire. I believe this dynamic occurs in the world of management consultants way too often. Check the degree, see the business school, look at the previous employers — but make sure you also check the humility, the humanity, and the motivation. Superstars will inevitably make the world revolve around themselves, and they will bring down the department if needed in the process.

Don't let yourself ignore my three rules of hiring! You know the circumstances. As a departmental manager, you may really need to fill the night operations position, and even though the candidates just aren't up to your normal standards, you settle for someone (this tends to be true more often when the job market is particularly tight). I did this once with a night operator, only to discover the person I'd hired was running a drug business on the side — making drops and picking up cash all through the night while his attention should have been on the nightly batch process. A few missed reports, some delayed backups, some downtime in the morning before the batch run finished, some blank spots in the written logs — it took awhile, but we finally put the pieces together and made a case. It's not too often that you get a chance to see an employee loaded into the back of a police car in handcuffs.

Assembling Teams

Hiring well is vital for IT departmental effectiveness; however, I believe having the right team members is just as important. Now, it's the rare IT leader who gets the chance to hire all members of every team. You've probably inherited some staff that came from the previous regime, or you've been assigned team members from other departments.

> *To have a chance to be the most effective IT leader possible, you need to have the ability to accept or decline the members of the team you take into battle with you.*

Okay, so what does this mean, exactly? To me, I return to my rules of hiring exceptional, skilled, accountable people and apply them to assembling teams. Instead of "hiring" someone on a team, I "assign" them to my team using the same criteria I use to hire someone in the first place. I remember someone from my past burning the following words into my head: Avoid creeping meatballism. Translation: Do not settle for meatballs when you need steak.

Continuing the food metaphor for a moment, I find great teams are like great meals. The right mix of flavors, textures, smells — and the right balance from the food group pyramid — leads to a healthy, satisfying, epicurean repast. Similarly, the right balance between roles and expected dynamics in your groups leads to successful results as a leader.

Group Dynamics

Further, it is critical to understand the roles played by team members and the associated group dynamics. Some might believe that the dynamics of teams don't have a high correlation to overall group success. I couldn't disagree more. Group dynamics can be predicted based upon the normal roles the participants prefer and the type of group being formed.

> *Great leaders have the ability to seed their teams with the right mix of personalities to ensure the highest possible chance for success. Poor leaders just expect the participants to get along and work through their issues with each other.*

I've been teaching a "Powerful Group Participation" workshop since the mid-90s, and here's the definition for dynamics I include in that session: Group dynamics is the interaction and interplay among group members. Additionally, group dynamics never ends (thus, the word dynamics!) and differs based upon the type of group involved:

Type of Group	**Major Goal**
Casual Groups	Play
Learning Groups	Intellectual Development
Cathartic Groups	Ventilation, Release
Policy-Making Groups	Establish Direction, Order
Action Groups	Implementation
Encounter Groups	Interpersonal Growth

We may have play-related groups at work, such as the company softball team, a bowling league, or a crafting group. However, some companies actually use play groups as part of their creativity and innovation process, and I think more departments and organizations could benefit directly by doing this more often. Obviously, in a work context, we probably don't assemble and lead groups related to catharsis or encounter situations (unless that's your business). Instead, most of our work-related groups involve learning, policy-making, or action.

> *We need to ensure we have the right people participating, with the right roles, and the right rules of engagement.*

While these issues are important in an intra-departmental sense, when looking at mixed groups of IT and non-IT persons, I've seen how paying attention to group dynamics and interpersonal interaction has paid huge dividends for me over the years. I have found this to be particularly true because IT tends to be misunderstood and too often unfairly judged by non-IT groups.

Additionally, role changes are common within different types of groups. For example, you may be the night operations shift supervisor in the computer room at work (a low-level management role) but be the founder and CEO of your own eBay-based business.

Forming and maintaining a group consists of several steps and components. Great leaders understand these steps and make sure they are handled proactively. As groups form, shift, and change over time, each of these steps is repeated. You may not be aware of it, but it happens — and I believe it's better to have your "hand on the wheel" as these dynamics play themselves out rather than leaving them up to chance.

- Communication Interaction

- Norm Setting and Evaluation

- Role Establishment

- Conflict Instigation and Resolution

- Productivity Sampling and Evaluation

- Consensus Taking and Appraisal

- Overall Satisfaction Judgment

Communication Interaction

This is the process of understanding how communication will occur within the group. Is it okay to have everyone talk over everyone else, or will this group have a moderator — someone responsible for managing the flow of communication? Think about your first meeting with your son or daughter's soccer or basketball team. You're the coach; it's up to you to establish the communication interaction pattern.

In my experience as a coach, I make sure the kids feel comfortable being able to ask questions — even to disagree with what they hear. However, they will do it in a respectful, polite, and considerate manner. I clearly state the process by which our communication interaction will be made. I also do this at work when I'm tasked to create a group to work on an IT-related project. I make sure they understand this process clearly.

Norm Setting and Evaluation

Different groups clearly have different norms. In a play group, you wouldn't expect to have to ask permission to speak. Conversely, in a policy-setting group, you wouldn't expect to see tissue boxes on each table as you would in a cathartic group. A common norm today in business-related meetings has to do with the policy concerning cell phones, pagers, PDAs, laptops, and other wireless devices.

My personal preference is to have short meetings (see Chapter 8, Calling and Running Meetings) where PDAs, cell phones, and so on aren't welcome. I'd rather have undistracted group participants for shorter periods of time. Setting norms — and discussing the evaluation of these norms — helps to bring a common understanding of how the group participants will behave and treat each other.

Role Establishment
The chart on the next page shows the most common roles I've found in groups of any kind. Establishing roles isn't something that most leaders spend much time doing, but it is where the group's ability to function at a very high level begins. As such, it is critical for the most effective leaders to "seed" their teams with individuals who play these following roles — and to leave room in the group dynamics for the role-playing to evolve and mature. However, a few words of caution.

It is rare to find a task leader who is also a social-emotional leader. Make sure you've got the right person in the right role. I'm clearly more of a social-emotional leader who can be a task leader, but I'm better at the former, not the latter. Also, choose your central negative role player with care. Often, this person is most responsible for the effectiveness of the group.

The chart on the following page describes "sub-roles" in groups that are often played by different people at different times. You know the silent observers — the people who don't say much, but when they do, it is usually profound. You wish these people would speak up earlier, but you are glad when they do. The active listener is another beneficial sub-role in that this person keeps the meeting from falling into boredom or passivity. The recorder role (secretary, minutes-taker) needs to be handled properly. If this is a permanent role in a group, it should be held by someone who isn't part of the group process. Otherwise, the recorder will feel disenfranchised, and their group-level esteem will diminish. Self-centered followers should be weeded out as quickly as possible. These people have no place in highly effective teams.

Most Common Group Roles	Behaviors, attitudes, actions
Task Leader	High group status, mature, good problem-solving skills, trained in leadership skills, extroverted, measures the productivity of the group. Feels responsible, experiences high pressure, leaves a leadership void when absent.
Social-Emotional Leader	Well-liked, good experience at handling interpersonal problems, can empathize. Responsible for the heartbeat of the group, sets the climate, looks for the satisfaction of each individual member.
Tension-Reliever	Humorous, but must be funny to all members of the group. Understands the sensibilities of the group, breaks up potentially debilitating interpersonal tension. Care must be given so this person is not interpreted as simply being a clown.
Data Provider	Accurate and concise information, instant availability, research skills, expert knowledge, usually a shared role among many members of the group.
Central Negative	Same skills as task leader, not happy with what is going on, challenges, evaluates ideas, makes an agenda, instigates conflict, dominates, blocks, usually creates positive results.
Questioner	Incisively probes without threats or alienation, seeks ideas and idea evaluation, clarification.

Again, the more attention a leader pays to these various roles during team assembly (and throughout the life of the team), the better the team's overall performance is likely to be.

Group Roles Not Often Played As a Separate Specialty	Behaviors, attitudes, actions
Silent Observer	Waits, listens attentively, listens to arguments passively, forms opinions. Quite often their decisions swing the group, not a role appreciated by the group members.
Active Listener	Non-verbal and supportive behavior, role shared among members of a successful group, remains argumentatively neutral but supports group members as they make input.
Recorder	If they must act as the recorder for long periods of time, they feel subservient. Some formal groups invite a non-member to act as recorder.
Self-Centered Follower	In it for his or her own gain, works against the best interests of the group, special interest support, lobbying for personal goals.

So far, we have talked about leadership roles within teams. Obviously, there are "follower-ship" behaviors that can positively or negatively influence the success of your team as well. Paying attention to these — rewarding the positive, and mitigating or eliminating the negative — will definitely improve the performance of your team.

Positive Follower-ship Behaviors:

- Listening attentively
- Assisting on procedure
- Observing
- Energizing
- Compromising
- Encouraging
- Recording

Negative Follower-ship Behaviors

- Dominating
- Blocking (foot dragging)
- Self-confessing (inappropriate catharsis)
- Help-seeking (sulking to get attention)
- Recognition-seeking (boasting)
- Special interest pleading
- Playing the clown (goofing off)

Outstanding Group Process Commitments

- Commitment to do individual best and to demonstrate only positive leadership and follower-ship roles
- Recognition of the role you play and the role others play
- Commitment to the group's good
- Commitment to be rational
- Commitment to fair play
- Commitment to good listening

Leading Teams

"You lead people, you manage things." Lt. General Chuck Horner

We need to make sure we don't confuse management and leadership — particularly in teams. And, not to rehash the second chapter, there are some specifics related to leading teams of people that I've found to be highly valuable and important. The most effective leaders of people are those who have the ability to see the bird instead of the egg. One of my favorite examples of such leadership is depicted in the Magritte painting entitled *Clairvoyance*. I'm not sure I like the title, but I love the painting.

Just like the painter in Magritte's painting, leaders can see the final people-related product before it's done. Project management, HR policies, and training manuals aren't about leading people. They are about managing things.

Too often, our business leaders misunderstand this point. People thirst to be led, not to be managed. As such, leaders bring hope, compassion, understanding, motivation, and clarity of direction to their teams.

If you are responsible for a team, ask yourself how much time you spend managing them as opposed to leading them. I remember a situation from my early career when I learned a big lesson related to the difference — and value — between management and leadership. I became the head of the IT department for a large company when I was quite young. Too young, probably, but that's another story. I became responsible for a multi-million dollar IT budget, a large staff, and technology implementations across the U.S. when I was the seasoned age of 23. Yow. Did I have some learning experiences ahead of me.

One thing I had learned by then was that departmental managers held departmental meetings (more about running meetings effectively in Chapter 8), and that's exactly what I did. I held meetings. My limited view on what these meetings should be about included status reports, budget updates, and application backlog prioritization. So, we started having meetings, and I managed the process. I set the tone, I read the agenda, I kept time, and I basically dictated the outcome of the meetings.

Unfortunately, I also encountered resistance. Outright mutiny, you might call it. I had someone challenge my authority on a regular basis during these meetings, and I found it downright insubordinate. I didn't understand what was going on right away; it took a few months. You see, there was one person in my department who wasn't looking for me to provide management; instead, she believed I wasn't the legitimate leader of the group. She was challenging my ability (and right) to lead, not the fact that the executives of our company had made me the manager of the department. I was confused about this and thought what she needed was more management.

> *An effective central negative figure on your team provides you an opportunity to discover things about yourself that you wouldn't have otherwise. Respected central negatives are worth their weight in gold.*

As the open debate continued in our departmental meetings between this staff member and me, my leadership credibility became suspect in more and more staff members' eyes. They began to look forward to the confrontations and were lining up behind their "favorite" during the battles. It got ugly. Again, I thought she just needed me to tell her what her role was and how to act in the meetings. I was dead wrong. Nothing I was doing was making it anything but worse.

That is, until one day when I figured out what to do. As I was sitting in my corner office (debating with myself about whether I'd done the right thing in accepting this job!), I had a moment of clarity. As I was preparing for yet another staff meeting, wondering what traps she would be laying for me, I realized something. My arguments with this person were highly productive. In fact, nearly each time our heated arguments had played out, the end results were better for it. The department overall (and the company as a result) benefited from our debating. Wow! I experienced an epiphany of sorts. What if we could come to consensus ahead of the staff meeting?

As a leader, I needed this person's input and perspective, and based upon her behavior and tactics, she felt strongly about sharing with me. I needed to put away my manager's hat and put on my leadership hat. That day, I decided to invite her into my office before the staff meeting and discuss the agenda with her in advance. What a difference! We had the chance to talk things out — just the two of us — and come to consensus before the staff meeting.

> *I discovered that I needed to see the bird instead of the egg — the end result with the people involved, and not just the traditional management process I had been following.*

That staff meeting (and all the others in the future) were never quite as animated, but they certainly were much more productive. The staff would look to me, then to her, as I discussed things related to the department. They would see the agreement in our body language and would feel much more confident that the right solution had been proposed. My role as manager had been cemented-in because I realized I needed to show some leadership to a key member of the staff. Don't confuse management with leadership. I did, and it just about cost me my job.

> *Sometimes your staff needs you to show leadership by supporting others in their need to lead. Real leadership involves fostering and nurturing leadership qualities in those around you.*

"The Big Secret" Regarding Teams

Over the past 25 years, I have been part of lots of teams — some highly effective, others dismally so. Without getting into detailed research in the fields of interpersonal communications, conflict management, group theory, and organizational psychology, I have come up with a simple formula that works nearly every time.

Great teams are made up of everyday people who have the ability to share a passion and commit to the larger purpose. I don't ascribe to the theory that the best individual performers are required to have the best teams. As I indicated earlier, sometimes those with the best pedigree, education, or experience are insufferable as members of a team. They may be great on their own, but that may be the best place to leave them — on their own.

Here are some more secrets related to great teams:

- Look for breadth of skill types.
  - Business, finance, marketing, IT infrastructure, developers, testing, training, project management.
- Look for team members with complementary skills.
  - The right mix of big idea types, pragmatists, process-focused, motivational, nurturing, information gathering, creative, devil's advocates.

- Fight fairly.

    o   Honor the system, respect the team members, and attack the situation, not the personalities.

- When it's over, it's over.

    o   Don't live in the past. Celebrate your successes, learn from your failures, and move on.

> *Give me a group of skilled, accomplished, and humble people, add some specific goals and objectives, mix well with respect and good listening skills, and they'll make me look like a great leader every time!*

Chapter 7: Handling Expectations
Bosses and Users

*E*xpectations will sink you or save you, depending on how you handle them. This is true in life, but the world of IT has a special need for excellence in expectation handling, and effective IT leaders must demonstrate adeptness in this area. IT leaders are squeezed between expectations coming simultaneously from many different directions: the business needs, personality projects from "those in power," your boss, your users, your staff, your peers, your shareholders, and other stakeholders. Making expectation handling even more interesting in IT is that novices (those with a home PC) believe everything in IT should work like their PC: fast, pretty, focused on serving the individual person — and if it crashes or hangs, just reboot! IT supports and connects everything and everyone. It's enough to drive you insane (or maybe I should say IT's enough to drive you insane!).

> *Effective expectation handling starts with respecting the fact that everyone is entitled to have expectations. Even users and bosses.*

Let's look at this "in the middle of everything" issue for a minute. I have a friend who is an architect, and one of the things he specializes in is office workflow and layout. We were at lunch sometime back and started talking about some challenges we face in our work lives. As we talked, we hit upon a strange connection between us in his role as an architect and mine as an IT effectiveness consultant. It turns out we both have to predict and manage expectations as we are exposed to the ebb and flow of business relationships and politics.

As we all know, expectations are rampant and obvious when it comes to visible things such as office space, furniture, parking spaces, and such. In his job as an office space architect, Steve has to worry about making sure so-and-so gets the "right" office, and that this department and that department have proper separation (or linkage) in the physical workspace. He finds out about who is really important, who thinks they are important, which department is getting along, which one isn't, and so on.

His work attempts to create flow, synergy, and linkage among people in a physical manifestation. As such, his work is clearly visible to those around him, and the resulting opportunities for expectation management are relatively obvious (just put the blueprint on the wall and stand back).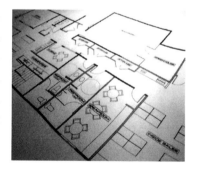

IT is similar in many ways except that we create the linkages between and among individuals, departments, business units, trading partners, regulatory agencies, institutions, external sources of data, and so on — but in a virtual sense. Our work isn't clear to the average person. Without a fairly deep background in IT architectures, commenting on whether one particular solution is best or not is often not advisable. Does that stop the average PC-literate type from offering his or her perspective? Not a chance. However, users, managers, and customers all have expectations of what they need from their IT architectures, even if they don't have the language to ask in a direct, concise, and technologically accurate manner.

Every human being has expectations — all of us. However, when we're in the heat of battle, and we're trying to get things done, it can be very difficult to stop and remind ourselves that we aren't the center of the universe. Everyone has expectations about outcomes, quality of life, budget, position, authority, control — you name it. If this is true, why is it that so many IT professionals expect their users and management to simply go along with whatever IT says? We need to stop that.

As I said at the outset of this chapter, expectations will save you or sink you. It all depends on the approach you take. You can let the people around you have whatever expectations they have, and then you can be measured against these random expectations. Or, on the other hand, you can play a role in helping to set proper expectations right from the start — and then have a chance to be measured against them instead. You decide. Remember, random expectations create unpredictable results, and unless you're a real thrill-seeker at work, you may want to be measured in a more predictable manner.

> *Proper expectation setting isn't a random thing. You must work to proactively create appropriate expectations.*

Think about this dynamic for a minute. When is it that you feel disappointed in life? It all has to do with your expectations not being met. Have you expected a raise or promotion in the past, only to be passed over? Did you feel disappointed? What about a time when you expected your spouse or partner to give you something for a special occasion, only to have them miss the mark in your eyes? More disappointment.

Missed expectations can devastate people; however, many times, the expectations are simply wrong. This is often the case with IT. As such, the most effective IT leaders are those who don't let expectations take their own course. Instead, these leaders work to set the expectations they want in the minds of those involved. There's a *big* difference in managing to the expectations *you* set versus being held to the expectations someone else comes up with for you.

With that as a backdrop, let's take a look at expectation handling in various situations: the relationship with your boss and the relationships with your users and staff members.

Expectation Handling with Your Boss

Having a high-quality relationship with your supervisor is an optimal situation, whether you work as a peanut vendor at the ballpark or with the CEO of a Fortune 10 company (yes, even CEOs have supervisors). A feature of a high-quality relationship with your boss must include proper expectation setting. Some might call this "managing your boss." Maybe there's some truth to that.

We've all run across ideas about managing your boss before — as if it's actually possible! While only a few bosses can be really managed, most bosses can at least be trained, particularly in expectation setting and handling. Some bosses will accept your overtures about training without hesitation or resistance. Others will need to be approached carefully before they'll accept training or managing from you. Each situation requires a customized approach.

Oh, I can hear the complaining now! Many of the bosses reading this are feeling slighted or somehow taken for granted. However, I am very serious. Training your boss about expectations is vital to being an effective leader, particularly in the world of IT.

I've had a variety of bosses over the years. Some have been great, others were useless, and one or two were so toxic that they should have required EPA hazardous material warnings. However, as an accountable IT leader, I found my relationships — even with the most dysfunctional boss — could be manageable if I worked hard to set proper expectations in their minds.

Let me ask you a few questions about the bosses you've had in the past:

- Which boss made you feel the most appreciated, involved, and successful?
- Which boss was a complete waste of your time?
- Which boss taught you the most about business? About yourself?
- Which bosses are you still on speaking terms with?
- Which bosses do you still look to for advice and guidance?

Think about your answers for a minute or two; it's likely you're thinking of those special, useless, dysfunctional, or poisonous bosses for the first time in years. However, each had an impact on you. Each gave you perspective either on how to be a great boss or on things *never* to do as a boss yourself. But, have you considered the role you played in the relationship with these bosses? Maybe a useless or poisonous boss could have been an ally if only you'd been more proactive in getting them to understand proper expectations.

Helping to set proper expectations in the minds of your bosses does not involve dodging issues, in hiding the facts, or in creating fear, uncertainty, or doubt in their minds. Instead, proper expectation setting has everything to do with being prepared, open, honest, and accountable.

I have a very good friend who is a CIO for a Fortune 500 manufacturing company. I remember being in his office on one occasion when the president of his company dropped by for a chat. It seems this president had just returned from a trip the night before, and he'd sat next to the regional sales manager for a PC company. Not being stupid, this salesperson "pumped" the president full of why he should have the latest Brand X laptop instead of the company-standard Brand Y laptop he had.

Anyway, the president had the brochure for "the" laptop he thought he wanted — full of the latest bells and whistles. During his chat, he mentioned to my friend that he wanted him to order this particular PC. Now, here's a chance to test your mettle as an IT leader. What would you have done in this situation? Would you have said, "Yes, Sir; absolutely, Sir"? I believe many of you would have. However, my friend took the chance to properly set expectations in the mind of his company president.

He said something like this:

> *"Do you really want me to get that laptop for you? If I get this one for you, it will violate the standard PC policy we implemented about three years ago. Also, because it would be for you, others would see you setting the example that exceptions to our "no exceptions on Brand Y" policy are okay. We've negotiated a very favorable purchase price and warranty policy with Brand Y PC vendor, and if you get Brand X, and others jump on board with your decision, I believe we'd end up spending at least another $100 K each year*

just to maintain a heterogeneous collection of PC platforms. I'll get it for you and deal with the ramifications with the user community if you decide you really want it. But, are you sure you really want that PC?"

I waited for that information to sink in with the president. In about three heartbeats, he said, "Oh, no. That's okay. My current laptop works just fine. Forget I mentioned it."

Now that's an example of effective expectation setting on behalf of an IT leader. My friend was prepared, open, honest, and accountable. In dollars and cents terms, he'd already estimated the potential outcome if someone like the president violated the PC mandate. He openly questioned the president's decision by asking if this is "what you really want me to do." He stated the facts as he knew them in a truthful manner, and he set the clear tone of accountability by saying that he would accept the president's decision, if he were forced to. My friend demonstrated the right approach to delivering business leadership in an IT-related situation by helping his president handle his expectations appropriately.

What would you have done in the same situation?

(As a postscript to this story, the president was subsequently fired, but the CIO still enjoys working for this same company. It seems some of the other "leaders" working for this president weren't quite so adept at helping him with his unreasonable expectations and went along with them. The company lost significant profits as a result of this president's unwise decisions.)

Expectation Handling with Your Users

User. A four-letter word to too many IT leaders. You know the attitude: "If those dang users would just leave us alone, we might actually get something done!" However, we need to remember that we're all users of IT solutions — each of us. Even the CIO of the world's largest company is a user of IT stuff. Even the most talented Java developer on earth is also a user. None of us can escape that label. Further, each of us was at some point a novice user of IT. I don't know too many people who just popped out of the womb and knew how to tune an Oracle database or write an Enterprise JavaBean.

Now, there are users, and then there are *users*! A small minority of users are just grumpy, crotchety, annoying pains in the neck, no matter what we do (that's true for people in general!). We all know it. And while most users are great most of the time, almost all users can be difficult users at times.

> *In my experience, almost all difficult users are disappointed users.*
>
> *Disappointment is a common, yet* controllable *human emotion usually stemming from unrealized expectations.*

IT is a fickle, imperfect thing. When Bill Gates's PC got the blue screen of death during a live demonstration of Windows 98's ability to recognize and configure devices on the fly, he said, "Even though we expect technology to work all the time, unfortunately, it doesn't." Gee. I guess even Bill Gates is a user!

Setting clear expectations with users is mandatory for an effective IT leader. The process is similar to what I shared with you about your boss: You need to be prepared, open, honest, and accountable. However, with users, you also need to be anticipatory and thorough in how you set expectations.

Setting Expectations

Here's a list of things to do to set proper expectations with users to help keep them on your side — and support you — as you work with them in designing and deploying IT solutions:

- Never assume a user understands the intricacies or details associated with a particular IT architecture, tool, or product. What's obvious to an IT person is often mysterious to a user.

- Keep the jargon, acronyms, and tech-head speak out of all user-related communication: training materials, presentations, memos, letters, e-mails, and so on.

- When explaining the time it takes to do something in IT, make sure users understand the steps needed in the process. Users don't inherently understand the need for things such as user interface design, integration testing, performance stress testing, documentation, and so forth.

    o Keep in mind that users believe everything "IT" should work like their personal computer.
    o As such, they completely underestimate the massive development time and costs associated with applications they buy and install on their PC.
    o Make sure they understand that custom applications built by your company (or your consulting firm) don't have multi-million dollar budgets — unless your company is Microsoft or IBM.

- Respect the fact your users are entitled to have expectations. I've said this before, but it bears repeating: Users are the reason IT exists, and IT leaders are keenly aware of this.

- Refer to Chapter 10, Measuring Your Effectiveness, for more tips on keeping users' expectations in mind as you deliver IT solutions.

What to Do When Expectation Setting Still Doesn't Work

Sometimes just working hard to set proper expectations isn't enough. No matter what you've done (I assume that you've followed good project management practices and have committed yourself to excellence in communication and all the other things I talk about in this book), those around you may still have unreasonable expectations of you, your group, or your department.

First, make sure the expectation to which you're being held is really unreasonable. I've witnessed many IT leaders who just don't want to do something. They don't like it, maybe because it's business oriented and not tech-head related. Sometimes IT leaders are asked to do things that aren't fun, interesting, or with any "resume-building" value. In all these situations, true IT leaders will take on the role of servant leader and will do what's necessary. Maybe the expectations of the IT leader need to be adjusted! Take a look and see what the right answer is in your situation.

> Beware the "must lose" scenarios. Some unscrupulous people may set you up to fail, no matter what you do. However, don't hide from difficult situations, either. Real leaders step in to fill gaps left by those who ran away.

However, there are times that "must lose" situations are presented by someone. I've seen situations in which budgets must be cut and the CFO mandates that all departments reduce their spending by some arbitrary percentage. "Cut your IT budget by 10 percent" you're told. And, at the same time, you're also told to make sure no one experiences any increases in downtime and that all software projects remain on schedule. "You're *nuts!*" you think to yourself — and you may even take the risk of telling your boss you think so. But still, no movement. You're still being held to the unreasonable expectation.

I have a simple answer in situations like these. Have integrity. Real leaders don't just buckle under when the opposition seems stacked against them; they don't just accept no-win situations. Strive to find creative alternatives; think outside the known limitations, and try to find a new set of expectations that can be realized. But never, never set up yourself, your company, your staff, your users, or your management to fail if you know their expectations cannot be met. Don't meet unscrupulous behavior with a lack of integrity. Just like the president I described earlier in this chapter, people who regularly ask for unreasonable things tend to find themselves as losers in the end.

Here's something that's on my wall at home, and I look at it every day. It helps me remember what's really important. (Yes, it's written using male gender terms, but I believe it is gender-neutral. I'd change it, but I'm not a good enough poet to fix it and still make it rhyme.)

The Man In the Glass

When you get what you want in your struggle for self
And the world makes you king for a day.

Just go to the mirror and look at yourself
And see what THAT man has to say.

For it isn't your father or mother or wife
Whose judgment upon you must pass.

The fellow whose verdict counts most in your life
Is the one staring back from the glass.

Some people may think you a straight-shootin' chum
And call you a wonderful guy.

But the man in the glass says you're only a bum
If you can't look him straight in the eye.

He's the fellow to please, never mind all the rest,
For he's with you clear up to the end.

And you've passed your most dangerous, difficult test
If the man in the glass is your friend.

You may fool the whole world down the pathway of years
And get pats on the back as you pass,

But your final reward will be heartaches and tears
If you've cheated the Man In The Glass.

Author Unknown

Chapter 8: Calling and Running Meetings
Preparation/Participation

*H*ow many times have you sat in a meeting feeling frustrated, anxious, irritated — and pleading silently for the person in charge of the meeting to run the dang meeting for goodness' sake? Or worse yet, you (and everyone else in the room, you can be assured) question the reason the meeting got called in the first place. Knowing when and how to call a meeting, and then effectively running the meeting, is one of the most important and effective things a good leader can know and do. Unfortunately, most IT (and business) leaders were absent during the class in which meeting skills were taught. Instead, they rely upon their positional leadership to be enough. "Because I said so!" doesn't work with parents, and it is even less effective for leaders.

Additionally, due to too many bad experiences with poorly run meetings, I think many of us have become cynical about meetings overall. Subsequently, through something called Neural Linguistic Programming (NLP, something Dr. Pavlov studied in detail through his work with sounds, dogs, and food), we often have a Pavlovian response to a memo announcing a meeting. "Oh, great. Another waste of time." I take a different view: I believe meetings can be informative, energizing, catalyzing, and motivating! Yes, I do. In fact, we've all attended meetings where we felt all these things, and I'll bet you were surprised when that happened.

It's all too common in the world of IT for our meetings to be perceived negatively. Why? Because by nature, most real business people have biases and misconceptions of what an IT-related meeting might be like. Too often, they believe the meeting will be full of techie-talk. (Okay, some of our IT brothers and sisters rely too heavily on jargon and "blinding BS" to communicate. We must all make a pact right now to stop that. *Stop* that. It doesn't make us look authoritative and intelligent; it makes us look annoying and conceited. *Stop that!*)

And, if the meeting is jammed with techie-talk, most real people either feel their participation is not necessary or that they will be forced to look stupid because they can't participate effectively. Either way, it's not a good thing for the IT leader. So, my overall advice related to effective IT communication is that we need to be extra careful to make sure we do not include buzzwords, acronyms, or jargon that the average person (I am thinking my aunt and uncle here) would understand immediately. *Never* assume anyone knows what something means. Bad form for sure, and debilitating, too, for IT leaders who want to be more effective at communication.

With that as a backdrop, let's look at some of the ways meetings can be good instead of bad.

Good Meeting Characteristics

- Have a clear agenda, and publish it in advance.
- Have a known purpose for the meeting.
  - If it is a standing meeting (like steering committees or staff meetings), have specific objectives for each meeting. Keep the overall agenda and process for standing meetings somewhat similar.
  - Understand that attendees want to know what to expect!

- o If the meeting is for information sharing, not brainstorming, limit the Q and A in advance.
- o If the meeting is for teambuilding and interpersonal sharing, do not set unreasonably firm or short time frames for meeting sections. Meetings of this kind need to evolve, and facilitators need flexibility.

- Set the "political tone" for the meeting as part of the agenda and advance materials.

  - o Give a complete list of attendees to all attendees, including those persons who may or may not be able to attend part or all of the meeting.
  - o Don't hide content related to organizational realignment or restructuring. If the meeting is to announce something of this kind, give as much advance notice and information about this as possible. In a vacuum, people do not assume good news.

- Appoint one person as facilitator.

  - o It may not be the most senior person in the room.
  - o The facilitator needs to have the clear authority of the most senior person, however, even if that person is not in the room!

- Start the meeting on time.

  - o Start on time even if everyone is not in the room. You need to establish this from the start; otherwise, just like kids, the participants will stretch the authority of the facilitator.
  - o Resume the meeting on time following breaks.

- Clearly communicate expectations of the meeting at the start of the meeting — including roles, responsibilities, and participation of each attendee.

- Allow only rare interruptions during the meeting.

  o Get rid of all distractions: cell phones, pagers, and PDAs.
  o Have a short, focused meeting rather than one that drags along due to interruptions.

- Make sure participants (speakers) are well prepared. This includes:

  o Dovetailing of messages
  o Consistency of terms
  o Similar look and feel to presentation materials (if part of the meeting)
  o Time frames that are respected

- Run sections of the meeting close to schedule, and handle any deviation in published time frames as they arrive.

  o Communicate dynamic schedule changes throughout the meeting, along with implications related to changes in ending times.
  o Understand that busy people are over-scheduled and as such are always mentally readjusting their time commitments.

- Summarize the meeting content at the end.

  o Note action items.
  o Share personal responsibilities and reach agreement.
  o Make clear the time frames, deadlines, and so on.
  o Set dates and times for any additional meetings.

- Prepare minutes shortly after the meeting, and circulate them among the attendees.

  o This is particularly important for policy-related meetings.
  o Everyone "hears" things differently, even with excellent facilitation and summarized content at the end of the meeting.

- o Minutes give attendees a chance to "hear the same thing, the same way" or to give feedback about the interpretation of the meeting content reflected in the minutes.
- o Allow attendees the chance to offer input and feedback about the minutes.

Unfortunately, I have few examples in my past of exceptionally good meeting leaders. I've built some cynicism surrounding meetings in general, and like most of us (I believe), I keep my expectations low so I don't become disappointed when the normally poor meeting dynamics manifest themselves. Every now and then, I'm pleasantly surprised when someone actually runs a good meeting. I always take the time and effort to thank the leaders of these meetings, and almost always, these leaders are surprised to have been recognized.

Bad Meeting Characteristics

The vast majority of meetings I have attended fit this category; they were just bad meetings.

- No agenda, or the agenda appears only at the beginning of the meeting, or worse yet, the "leader" of the meeting keeps the agenda to him or herself, referring to it by themselves, keeping it from everyone else.

- Vague or unknown purpose for the meeting.

  - o Even if it is a standing meeting (like steering committees or staff meetings), the process and content of the meeting changes, is random, or is predictably unpredictable.

- Because there are no advance materials, including no list of attendees, no one has a clue about who will be there and what the political ramifications and characteristics will be.

- o Frustration, cynicism, protectionism, positioning. In a vacuum (particularly related to personal power), people will almost always make negative assumptions.

- Random meeting leadership (oh, whichever executive happens to be there).

- Meetings starting late, running late, speakers unprepared, no coordination related to content or look and feel, and on and on.

You get the picture. While it took some thinking on my part, I was able to put one person in the category of "worst meeting leader in the history of the world." This person was so self-absorbed that she wouldn't even attend her own meetings on a regular basis. Most of the time, she would send some ineffectual underlings to express her perspectives and positions — without, of course, empowering them with the ability to say yes to anything. If she did grace us with her presence, she'd spend the majority of the meeting staring at her laptop, answering her seemingly endless stream of e-mails. She'd claim to be listening and would even occasionally growl some disagreement to a point being made. In general, she gave everyone the impression that she was just too good for the meeting — and for the people attending it.

As such, while she (I believe) felt like she was being the big, bad boss, most people despised her and looked for every opportunity to secretly sabotage her. She was a joke, and she didn't know it. Now, that's really sad. She probably still doesn't know it, as she's still working her "meeting magic" for a large company based here in Denver.

Want to stand out in the crowd? If you follow the rules for good meetings regularly and religiously, your "followers" will begin to look to you as a consistent, reliable, and respected/respectful leader. On the other hand, if you do not run good meetings, your credibility as a leader suffers dramatically (even if you are a good person otherwise). Effectively calling and running meetings gives real leaders the chance to demonstrate their skills and to reinforce their ability to lead. If nowhere else, new or emerging IT leaders — through their ability to run effective meetings — have the chance to grow themselves and to increase their sphere of influence as professionals.

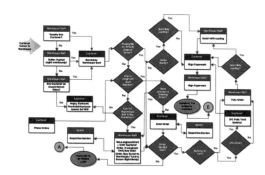

Chapter 9: Leading Projects
Fighting Human Nature

*H*uman-based projects never work exactly the way we expect them to work; they almost never come in exactly on time or exactly on budget, and they rarely deliver exactly against the requirements set out at the project inception. Instead, projects nearly always "fail" — within some tolerance — when measured in objective, cold, MS-project–based terms. Why? Basic human nature, that's why. That said, driving meaningful projects toward completion is the essence of what IT leaders are supposed to do. We are tasked with getting things done, and usually these things are in the form of projects.

Rest assured this chapter does not simply regurgitate the classic Project Management Methodology evangelized by organizations such as the Project Management Institute (PMI; www.pmi.org). Instead, I discuss some of the hidden secrets to successful project leadership, as well as some of the more common pitfalls. By the way, the PMI is a great organization that has a definite value proposition. However, this book is about leadership — not management — and much of what is included in the PMI trainings and certifications has little, if anything, to do with leadership. Further, I expect you have some familiarity with project management — the tools, the practices, and such. This chapter is not about how to put together a work breakdown structure or how to re-plan resources in an MS project.

What is the difference between project management and project leadership? Here is a concrete example. Project managers are measured by their ability to deliver the project using the resources, timelines, and tools available to them. That's it. Delivering projects to completion is also part of the responsibilities of a project leader; however, project leaders will also stop projects that need to be stopped, when the project needs to be stopped. This is a risky proposition for sure, but a necessary one. Too many projects seem to continue far beyond their usefulness.

Maybe the project sponsor has retired, or been replaced, or has been reassigned to a different department. Maybe the business need for the project is irrelevant now. Maybe no one anywhere can remember why the project was started in the first place. In any case, real IT leaders will stop wasting company or organizational resources on projects that should be stopped, even if it means asking difficult, unpopular questions. Some projects should fail — and quickly. A project leader keeps the business goals in mind, and if a certain project is not destined to deliver real results, the leader will kill the project. Red light.

> *Project management tools and practices are important components in keeping a project on track, but without focused and effective leadership, all the project management in the world won't keep the project from failing.*

Determining whether a project should or should not continue is part of the art of leading projects successfully. Being able to make that decision requires information, the ability to sort through alternatives, clear communication, and then the willingness and courage to take action. Again, this goes far beyond the project schedule.

Projects of any size are made up of hundreds or thousands of tasks, resources, milestones, and schedules. Keeping just the project details on track is an enormous undertaking; add in the random nature of human beings, and it is a wonder that projects get done at all. I believe the most successful project leaders are those who listen before speaking, who teach instead of demand, and who work toward delivering business results, not toward achieving political points.

There's a legendary story from western Colorado, in the town of Fruita to be specific. One day as a devoted son was carefully cleaving the head of a rooster just the right way (the rooster was destined to be his and his mother's dinner, and she loved chicken necks as long as they were cut "just so"), something unexpected and bizarre occurred.

Being a good son, he always tried to satisfy her desires to preserve the neck, and as a result, he became adept at doing it the way she liked. Anyway, after separating the head from the body of this particular rooster, the man was astonished at what happened next. Instead of bobbing and weaving for a few minutes, and eventually just falling over dead (like all the other chickens he'd decapitated), this chicken kept going. And going. And going some more.

In fact, this particular rooster became famous. Known as "Mike the Headless Rooster," he lived for about eighteen months — with constant water and food being dropped through his esophagus by his devoted caretakers. Does Mike remind you of anything? To me, Mike is an excellent metaphor for many projects within organizations. As managers come, and managers go, some projects just continue to live on without their heads. As long as someone is willing to drop food or water (money) into the "necks" of these projects, they continue — regardless of whether the project will ever bring value to the business. This is a ridiculous waste of resources and something a real leader wouldn't condone. Again, mature and effective IT leaders take the time to understand and evaluate the value of continuing a project. The "Mike Projects" of the world must die.

Communication

Quick quiz. What do you consider the most important trait of a quality project leader? Attention to detail? Tenacity? Focus? No, no, and no. These are all important, but to me, the most important quality effective IT project leaders have is their ability to communicate effectively. We've already talked about calling and running meetings (this is very important to project leaders) and the process of handling expectations (again, critical to project leadership). However, strong IT leaders need to exhibit other communication traits when it comes to projects:

1. Report, don't editorialize.

2. Give bad news using straight talk.

3. Under-promise, over-deliver.

Project-related communication should not over-explain, make excuses, assign blame, make political remarks, or otherwise editorialize on the situation. Status reports should discuss milestones reached, tasks accomplished, remaining workload, and overall project concerns or threats. Status reports are not a platform to vent personal gripes or to heave mud at stakeholders. Further, you will be measured as a project leader by your ability to communicate effectively and appropriately.

Remember, all projects will fail to some extent. It's expected. However, many of us in the world of IT are real people-pleasers at heart (at a minimum), and some of us are down-right panicked at the thought of any conflict. As such, too often, when we have bad news to report, we use the wrong language. Bad news is just that — bad news. It shouldn't be looked at as an indictment of one's personal worth! I will look at conflict more deeply later in the chapter; however, the point here is this: Bad news *always* happens in a project. Expect it. However, make sure to use the right approach when describing the bad news, and handle any conflict that arises.

> As the old saying goes, there's a time and a place for everything. Make sure your project-related communication respects and reflects this.

You can communicate bad news effectively if you follow the formula. First, you need to understand your audience. Are you delivering bad news to a supervisor, to an executive, to a group of users, a vendor, a contractor? Each of these audiences has different needs related to hearing bad news; make sure you use terms and language appropriate to the audience.

Second, make your introductory statement sound almost positive in nature. In other words, use something like this: "As our project moves forward, we continue to make progress in many areas." This statement gives the reader information about the positive forward direction. Following your introductory positive statement, give the specifics about the bad news. Sentences like this might work: "However, our progress has been impeded by a lack of buy-in related to funding options by the major stakeholders in our project." This gives the bad news in a direct, yet "non-attacking" manner.

Finally, when delivering bad news, make sure the audience is given the chance to understand potential ramifications or repercussions related to this bad news. Use something like this: "Should this lack of agreement persist beyond our deadline of April 17, we run the risk of missing the entire project deadline. Each day beyond April 17 in which we lack agreement will result in a 1:1 increase in the overall project schedule." This is clear, concise, and complete. Anyone familiar with the project will understand what needs to be done, by when, and what will happen if it doesn't happen. Remember, report — don't editorialize — and give bad news using straight talk.

The final requirement for effective communication — under-promise and over-deliver — needs to be manifested in all phases of project-related communication. From project inception (make sure you understand exactly what the expectations are at the beginning!) all the way through to close-out, an effective project leader will make sure expectations related to under-promising and over-delivering are consistently followed. This is particularly important in the world of IT, where most non-IT types do not have a strong understanding of what to expect from IT-based deliveries. Project leadership is all about project communication.

> *Excellent communication within a project team, and among project stakeholders, will often overcome even the most complicated, political, and challenging project environment. Communicate clearly, and your value as an effective leader will be indisputable.*

Communication Etiquette

- If you leave a message on voice mail, talk clearly. Give your return number in the first 10 seconds. Make your message short but complete. Repeat your return number at the end.

- Don't assume people know how to spell your name, and *never* assume you know how to spell someone else's. If you don't know, find out. Misspelling someone's name can be the kiss of death in building trust. Good spelling overall is just good communication. Bad spelling hints at sloppiness and unprofessional behavior.

- Always return your calls as promptly as possible. If you say "I'll be back in touch within four business hours," you'd better live up to this promise, particularly as a project leader. You are expected to lead by example.

- Honestly screen your calls; don't hide behind phone mail, and don't ask your administrative assistants to lie. Further, don't allow cell phones, pagers, PDAs, or laptops to interrupt meetings.

- Be aware of how you sound on the phone or in your e-mail. If you're too busy to pay close attention, your tone, inflection, and quality of communication will come through. Nobody likes to feel as though they are imposing on you, and if you give the impression of being too busy, you'll soon be looked at as unapproachable. A corollary to this advice:

- Remember, there's no substitute for a look in the eye and a handshake. Real people need contact with other real people. Make sure you spend as much time as practical in actual contact with members of the project team. Also, find out the preferred way of communicating with project stakeholders. Everyone is different.

Political Situations

"Politics" is a neutral term. By definition, it is neither positive nor negative; it just relates to the rules of human interaction. However, we all know that politics often is mysterious, painful, and ugly — where the average IT professional is a loser right from the start. Too many IT types are quiet, shy, and reserved and would rather have their gums scraped before stooping to any political game-playing. Fair enough.

However, winning at politics does not mean you need to resort to underhanded, unscrupulous activities or behaviors.

Assuming the project is delivering real business value, responsible and mature project leaders know when and how to use politics to the advantage of their project.

Good political game-playing can make project success simpler, faster, and more effective. On the other hand, most dysfunctional political situations involve win/lose situations in which someone uses their positional authority, their relationships, or their organizational power to make someone lose. Good politics is all about win/win. As such, the next time you find yourself faced with a political situation, take a look at this list of helpful tips related to good politics.

- Beware of, and be aware of, rivalries among persons, departments, or divisions. Know what you are getting yourself into. Ask questions about the history, the mythology, and the "unwritten rules" associated with political situations. Ignorance is no excuse.

- The more balanced your perspective, the more balanced your attitude. If you are secretly hiding resentment, fear, or hostility, you will find it difficult to be motivated to play positive politics.

- Your level of investment directly affects your level of political risk/ involvement/needs. If you are about to retire, you are highly unlikely to take much risk. On the other hand, if you are willing to look at the overall situation as if you "owned" the outcome yourself, your investment level will be substantial.

- You do not, absolutely do not, have to continue working in politically dysfunctional and/or unsatisfying situations. If you cannot create a win/ win situation, no matter what you try, give yourself permission to leave the situation. Then, be accountable to yourself for this permission.

- You can let politics seize you up, you can seize it, or you can get lost in the shuffle. Things change, people change, situations change. Keep yourself attuned and open to the ever-evolving situations within your organization. Then, keep your head on straight vis-à-vis the political situations. Lead, follow, or get out of the way (as the old saying goes). Don't just stand there whining!

- Finally: Communicate directly. Don't get caught up in the need for power. Be a positive role model. Speak from an informed, confident position. Do not be defensive.

Is This Estimate Padded?

This is the question no project leader really wants to answer honestly. We all know it is common to pad estimates, either in terms of time, or money, or both, when putting together a project schedule. We use fancy words like "contingencies" when describing the areas of the project in which we're either clueless or someone is unwilling to take accountability for outcomes. However, let's return to Chapter 1. Today's IT success is based largely on the fact that business leaders are holding IT leaders accountable for ROI — whenever and wherever possible.

> *Openness in project-related communication is very disarming. Most executives expect to hear only good news or marketing-spun, sugar-coated reports about problems. By being open in your communication, you build trust.*

If you pad the estimate, be open about it. Doing this disarms any potential distrust project stakeholders may have. Remember, the average non-IT person doesn't inherently trust the word of an IT person. But by coming clean about contingencies, I have found it creates a climate of openness and honesty directly from the start of the project. The non-IT folks may still not necessarily understand the project communication, but they believe it.

Conflict

Another critical skill that separates the great leaders from the not-so-great has to do with instigating and resolving conflict. Great leaders know that great teams provide for conflict; in fact, the more successfully a group can instigate and resolve conflict often translates directly into how effectively the group works together. Without conflict, the group process atrophies, and relationships become weakened. Just like polite neighbors on a small island, a group that doesn't own up to its conflict will ultimately resort to gossip, innuendo, rumors, and overall dysfunction in its approach to resolving differences. However, most of us have never taken the class on conflict instigation and resolution. Instead, we hope the other person will back down or the conflict will just resolve itself. This happens only on television.

Exacerbating the conflict conundrum is the fact that most IT professionals will avoid conflict at all costs. As a group, we tend to be introverted, shy, socially restricted, and risk avoidant. These facts don't bode well for our ability to deal with conflict. Measuring your effectiveness as an IT leader means you need to get over this shortcoming. Conflict in business doesn't necessarily translate into personal conflict. This isn't the playground in second grade where someone tells you that they don't like your hair, your glasses, or your shoes.

> Here is a big secret I have learned over the years about conflict. Say this to yourself five or six times in a row: "I can be right, or I can be happy." I am amazed at the number of people I know who have to be right at the expense of their relationships, their health, and their mental well-being. So what about .NET or J2EE? Who cares? Both standards will win. Get over it.

Instead, a business-related conflict may involve opinions of priority, or urgency, or funding, or business-related value. If all members of the team have the best interests of the overall organization in mind, conflict will give the team new avenues to explore and new potentialities to examine. It will build depth and substance to possible outcomes. Again, I firmly believe differences of opinion need to come forward.

After all, conflict is needed in relationships. It is the spice that brings out the best flavors in the team interaction. Remember the story about my central negative in Chapter 6? Learning to value and understand the conflict this person brought into my life, in a positive manner, was a massive turning point in my maturation as a leader.

Lessons Learned

During the dot-com boom, I found myself agreeing to assist a client with a project that was definitely a mess. The story goes something like this. I was asked to "fix" a very large project that was clearly out of control. In fact, our client had for all intents and purposes fired us — and then realized they were stuck with us as their only choice to get the project done. I came in about halfway through the entire project duration, just past the point when the project requirements and business cases had been prepared and just as the actual detailed design of the solution was beginning. The project entailed a combination of client staff and consultants in four different cities and three time zones.

> *When things go sideways in a project, you have two choices. You can be right — and hide behind schedules, status reports, project charters, or other project documents to "prove" you're right — or instead, you can be a project leader and look for ways to create real value for the business or organization.*

The situation was clear. It was early January, and the client had set an early March installation time frame. We had to meet the time frame or run the risk of not being able to collect our fees. What would you have done during your first hours, days, or weeks on this project? If you approached it like a project manager, you would have dug into the schedule — looking at to-dos, at resources, at accountabilities, and at time frames. I didn't do that. I approached it like a project leader. I needed to assimilate as much as possible of the project situation as quickly as possible. I needed to understand the essence of why we'd been "fired" by this client.

Making matters even more interesting were these dynamics: This project was for a major corporation that had just been formed about nine months previously. Additionally, there had been just about zero done on business process optimization or even coordination between the two legacy organizations that were jammed together to create the new business.

Our project was to consolidate the three product offerings of this new organization into one e-commerce site and effectively price, order, and deliver the products throughout the U.S.

Oh, and some more information to add to the mix: The company for whom I was working had just been formed about nine months earlier itself, and we were nowhere near complete with our business process change. As such, the three different parts of our business that were working on the project for our client had very different approaches to delivering projects. In fact, one part sold the project (badly, I might add), leaving the other two parts of the business with impossible expectations (remember those from Chapter 7?).

> *This project was a disaster from the start, and if the project leaders had been thinking clearly and objectively, they would not have taken on the project. But at times, the need for revenue clouds even the best person's judgment.*

Getting to the Heart of the Matter

Anyway, rather than digging into the documentation associated with the project's charter, schedule, resource table, and such, I looked for ways in which the project could be successful, in spite of the difficulties at hand. I met with the client, I met with our team, and through these conversations, two things became clear.

- First, being right about the internal differences in our team's approaches to delivering work (methods, revenue sharing, and so on) was *far* more important to our internal team than were the objectives of meeting our client's expectations. That had to change.

- Second, the client thought they could simply abdicate (the word they used was "outsource") the project to a consultant and therefore eliminate their accountability. Just pay the bill, and expect your contractor to do everything for you. Wrong.

Once the ship was righted, and our team was "encouraged" to stop thinking internally (okay, threats worked pretty well here!) — and the business side of the client was also "encouraged" to actually make real business decisions about their project — we started to make progress. Ultimately, the project was completed, and the client paid the bill.

Staying on Purpose

At the risk of upsetting everyone who has read this far, I'm going to make a couple of generalizations about techie-types. First, we tend to be easily distracted. The latest, greatest thing gets our attention, and we can lose focus on what we've already committed to do. Second, many IT types tend to be socially nervous and have more than an average need to be liked by their fellow human beings. I'm not sure these characteristics are limited just to techie-types; I've met a lot of people who are easily distracted and who want to be liked.

However, for an effective IT leader, being easily distracted and having an unreasonable need to be liked can be killers for project success. And these are not the only project killers. IT projects also tend to suffer from a lack of alignment with corporate or business goals. This usually manifests itself in poorly defined scope (the tech part is understood, such as which database, development tool, security monitor, middleware application, or messaging architecture will be used) because the real business goals are not clear.

Considering the fact that most projects are destined to fail — by purely objective measures — and that IT leaders are measured by the results of our teams, it is clear that effective leaders have mastered the ability to communicate, predict, mitigate, innovate, and deliver through their teams. Going it alone means you sink by yourself.

Chapter 10: Measuring Your Effectiveness
Facilitating, Assisting, Serving

*M*easuring effectiveness. This sounds like a simple thing, really, and many organizations attempt to develop the ultimate scorecard that's objective, clear, and unambiguous. Entire organizational reward programs are often built as a result of these measurement systems, and millions of people worldwide devote themselves to delivering against them. Unfortunately, much of this time is wasted when it comes to truly measuring your effectiveness as a leader.

I remember a time in my own life. About six or seven years ago, my wife and I finally made the decision to finish the basement in our house. We'd purchased a house with a walkout basement — with a nice view across a "wild" area — and had been planning for years to make the lower level into a real part of the house. One consequence of this decision was that we would no longer have to share an office. If you know us at all, you'll know this was a good decision, as our approaches to managing working space are totally different. So, I got my new office in the basement, and the study just off the main entrance of the house became Debi's office alone.

Nearly simultaneously with the completion of our basement remodel, I found myself with the need to work from home. Now more than just a home office for me, this was my primary workspace — and it gave me the chance to bring the stuff I had at my real office and put it up on the walls and on the shelves. Once the real office to home office switcharoo was completed, there I was, sitting in my new office surrounded by all the things I felt were important to me and my value as a professional. Debi did the same thing with her office (of course, it took *much* more time to coordinate the colors and textures in the room; her office just looked better overall!).

> Make sure you use the right measures when adding up your success or when measuring your effectiveness. Too often we use pop-culture criteria, the equivalent of using Twinkies to measure nutrition.

Once we were both finished with our offices, I took the opportunity to stand back and compare. That's when it hit me: She and I had very different views on measuring our effectiveness. It was as obvious as the stuff on the walls and shelves. What was in Bob's office? I had framed copies of the most meaningful awards and achievements I'd received. "In recognition for …" "In appreciation of …" The walnut and gold veneer outlining the fake sheepskin and computer-generated calligraphy images were everywhere.

I also had many engraved pieces — clocks, plaques, and such — that were three-dimensional testaments to my professional effectiveness. Dates, places, groups — I had a visual chronology of my awards, accomplishments, and achievements. Cool.

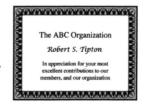

The ABC Organization

Robert S. Tipton

In appreciation for your most excellent contributions to our members, and our organization

Then I took a look at Debi's office. What did she place on the walls and the shelves? Oh, something very different. Instead of impersonal testaments and documents, she had pictures of how she measured her effectiveness. Smiling back at her from their vantage points in her office were pictures of me and of the kids.

Bang! Sometimes the 2x4 that hits you in the head leaves a mark. Here's the lesson I learned that day: Don't measure your leadership effectiveness through personal accomplishments or awards received; instead, measure it in the eyes of those you lead.

> *Just like great parents measure themselves as parents through the words of teachers, coaches, neighbors, ministers, rabbis, and others who have deep and intimate relationships with their kids, a real leader measures him or herself by the accomplishments and achievements of those whom they lead.*

Reading the Tea Leaves

As a consultant, I've been trying for years to "formula-ize" the process of looking at an organization's IT architectures, culture, and spending to get a read on the health and well-being of the overall organization itself. Read the "tea leaves" of the IT organization, and you'll be able to understand the effectiveness of the business. An analogy might be measuring a person's individual effectiveness by looking at their checkbook. Do you balance your checkbook regularly? Do you know at any given point in time just how much money you have? Are you operating against some budgetary guidelines in your personal spending? Examining the status of someone's checkbook can tell you a lot about that person's state of mind, what's important to them, and so on. The same can be said about an organization when looking at its IT architecture and the departmental organization.

Remember, IT leaders (going all the way back to Chapter 2) play a proactive role in assisting their organizations in understanding the benefits and trade-offs of various IT-related options. Real IT leaders didn't let their companies waste millions on dot-com stuff when there was dubious business benefit. Real IT leaders teach, compare, suggest, cajole, prod, and recommend — all the time — about innovations in IT and how these innovations can be leveraged to support real problems.

Is your IT organization set up to assist your users in making decisions and in charting a course through the glut of information overload they experience? Have you fought and won the battle for funding related to business intelligence applications, data warehouses, and executive decision support systems?

Does your IT architecture foster integration between and among departments, divisions, and trading partners? Do you champion the adoption of tools that lead to flexibility, nimbleness, and adaptation in business direction? Answering yes to questions like this tells me that you would receive high marks as an IT leader.

> *Examine the quality of strategic, business-related uses of IT within your organization, and you'll be able to measure the effectiveness of your IT leadership.*

If, on the other hand, your IT organization pushes your company to keep technologies and tools that support the resumes of the IT staff, or your staff holds the company hostage for salary, benefits, working conditions, and such due to the fact that only a few key individuals actually know how the systems are put together, or if your IT organization begrudgingly accepts business-related projects on the condition that the tech-heads will get some new technology or training in return, you will receive low marks as an IT leader.

Keeping Their Confidence

Obviously, being a leader means you need someone to follow you, but good words of caution for leaders are these: Occasionally turn around and look behind you to see whether anyone *is* following. Too often, leaders just assume their followers are still there (mentally, emotionally, physically, and intellectually). And, just as often, the followers have moved on. Why? Many reasons. First, those who were following you may have lost confidence in your leadership abilities. Many naïve and inexperienced managers believe they should just be followed because they have "manager" in their title. Supervisory job descriptions alone are not a license to lead.

Second, going back to Chapter 2, remember that leadership is something given, not something taken. Those we lead give us permission to lead them; they accept us, not the other way around. Great leaders honor this dynamic and regularly measure their effectiveness by looking at the depth and quality of relationships they have with those whom they lead. Further, don't assume you know what others perceive about you or your leadership ability. If you don't know, ask.

Here are a few questions a great leader will ask of those he or she is leading (and not just once a year at the HR-mandated annual review; great leaders ask all the time):

1. What most motivates you to feel accepted, encouraged, and empowered?

2. What barriers exist in our relationship or your working situation that get in the way of these motivations?

3. Am I serving your current needs fully so that you are able to get your job done as effectively as possible?

4. How can I assist you in reaching your long-term personal and professional goals?

> *Great leaders lead their followers from where the followers are, not where you want them to be. No jumping through hoops required.*

How do you feel about asking these questions? Great leaders — no matter the context — will ask and act upon these kind of questions. I am convinced the greatest leaders in my life have had exactly these motivations for me. However, do not ask these questions if you are not ready, willing, and able to follow through with action. Simply hearing requests or motivations like these — without doing something about them — is the equivalent of giving someone a brand new Porsche without giving them the keys. It's cruel and manipulative. More importantly, it will completely undermine any confidence your followers have in your leadership. They will leave you.

Final Thoughts

Again, find ways to gain satisfaction and meaning through the efforts and accomplishments of those whom you lead. Their successes (based upon their special gifts and talents) are to be celebrated, not evaluated through an expectation filter based upon the words "should" and "ought." Going back to the parental metaphor for a moment, I urge you to be the parent your daughter or son needs you to be, not the parent you think you should be. What a difference this would make for the teenagers (and employees) of the world! They don't need us to judge and correct them; they need us to meet them right where they are and lead them forward from there.

Be the leader your followers need you to be, not the manager that your job description tells you to be. Be the leader your business needs for IT decision-making and strategic thinking, not the tech-head your resume wants you to be. It will be at that point that you will be able to say to yourself with complete confidence, "I am an effective IT leader." Believe it, act upon it, and it will become true.

> This simple shift in thinking pays huge dividends on both sides of the relationship. However, in order to get there, it means you have to get over yourself, and that's often the most difficult thing a person can do. Get over yourself. You are only important as a leader if those whom you lead are important.

A Few Last Words
Real-Life Untangled Stories

*U*ntangling IT is certainly a tall order, and I hope this book has offered you some practical and down-to-earth insights for being an effective IT leader. Obviously, there is much more related to effective IT leadership than I included here. So, like Indiana Jones, maybe there are other adventures to come!

As I was putting this book together, I handmade about 75 copies and distributed them as preview copies. The only expectation I had of those to whom I gave the book was to give me some feedback and some stories. I received some amazing feedback (mostly positive, but not all. After spending seven years as an opinion columnist, I'm used to getting mixed reviews!) and some great stories. A few of those are included here.

If you have any personal tips about effective IT leadership or stories in which you learned a great lesson, let me know! I will include them here as I print new editions of this book. That way, this last chapter can become a living resource to all future readers — and maybe, just maybe, if I get enough "kitchen-table wisdom" about effective IT leadership, you might see a separate collection of those stories, too! (Yes, I will get your permission, and there might even be a fabulous cash prize. Well, maybe it would be fabulous to a 10-year-old, but to you, it might mean dinner out!)

Anyway, thanks for reading. I look forward to hearing back from you.

Bob Tipton
2003

feedback@rstipton.com

Untangled Anecdotes

I think it's important to emphasize the "IT armchair quarterback syndrome." Everyone thinks they understand the world of IT, all through their own personal experience with their comfortable little PC in their home office late at night, when the reality is no one really understands the changing world of IT, not even those of us in the world of IT, and we "get it" better than most. Everyone believes that business systems should behave just like your PC applications — simple little icons, everything looks similar, intuitive, always does what you want (for the most part), and happens quickly (no waiting for system resources or long reports to run).

More important is my long-standing belief that our customers always remember the last thing you did for them along with all the things you haven't done yet. When it's all said and done, I've always believed that every decision I make regarding IT is wrong — eventually. I'm just trying to be the least wrong.

Larry Shutzberg, CIO, Rock-Tenn Company

Early in my IT management career, I was hell-bent on getting a new application installed by a certain deadline. As the implementation date grew near, my staff approached me and advised me to delay the cutover, as there was no possible way it could be ready in time. I didn't respond well to their input, probably because I knew they were right but had been too proud to "face the music." I delayed the implementation but lost some of their respect because of the way I reacted.

Similar situations have arisen since then, and armed with a little more experience and confidence, I've been able to relieve some of the undue pressure people put on themselves when unavoidable project delays occur. I tell them, "If a new system goes in smoothly, people will soon forget that the implementation was delayed. But if rushed in before it's ready, users will remember the pain for a long, long time."

Dwight Gibson, CIO, Leprino Foods

Addressing the issue of poor performance is very problematic for IT leaders. What I've seen is that managers either dance around the issue or drop hints about unsatisfactory performance but can't, or won't, be direct. Since most IT personnel are guys, dropping hints and skirting the issue is not at all effective! Firing for all but the most blatant offenses does not seem to occur. Rather, they wait until budget cuts and then use that excuse to get rid of the poor-performing employee.

Carol Woodbury, Co-Founder, Skyview Parnters

I cannot over-emphasize the importance of a good team. I once worked on a project where management had added a new hire to our project team. After a few months, it became obvious (to me, at least) that this person was dragging down the whole project. After further analysis, I determined that, for every error that he "fixed," on average, he inadvertently introduced two new errors. This was basically due to incompetence; he was not cut out to be a programmer. He could not manage the details at all.

This set our project back, we missed our QA target dates, and the whole project slipped by six to eight weeks because of just this one person. It was only after I convinced management to move him off our team and assign him to something (anything!) else that we were able to complete the project and deliver the next release of this application.

(Name withheld by request)

I think IT leaders need to reflect on using business sense rather than IT sense. For example, in contingency planning for disasters, having a hot site that can get IT up and running in 24 hours is a tempting (easy way out?) way for IT to cover itself. But does it make business sense to pay a gazillion dollars for something that in all likelihood will not happen, when it is known that the business would be able to limp along in manual mode for the one to two weeks it takes for IT to be come functional again, and it is known that the business could sustain this kind of outage with little loss in cash flow or market share? Obviously this thinking doesn't apply to all businesses, but I think I can make a good case for the trash business.

Dave Burbank, CIO, Western Disposal

In the early 80s, one of the original founders of a major engineering company where I worked published a Little Yellow Book that contained a collection of thoughts on how to run a business and how to be as a person. One of his thoughts was, "Approve computerization only if it will be beneficial at twice the estimated costs or if bankruptcy can be avoided when the cost runs five times the estimate." This thought was assembled in 1980 when the company had just completed a DEC 10 conversion and we had some "unfortunate" things happen. An interesting additional story is that we converted to an Oracle system in 1995 — and one of the results was we lost our entire accounting system for five full months (we nearly went bankrupt).

Dave Ellison, Founder and CEO, SynergyConnects

I agree with all you've said about effective (servant) leadership. The best manager I ever worked for had a book on her shelf called *101 Ways to Reward Your Employees*, or something like that, and she really took the idea to heart. She always worked to help us do our jobs better. She came up from the programming ranks but also understood the business side and communicated well, so she was a good go-between for the techies and the rest of the company.

She made sure we got training whenever we could, and she let us be involved in deciding what training would best suit our and the department's needs. She tried to provide small perks whenever possible, such as Day-Timers each year, including a leather cover if you needed one. One thing I learned from her was to never underestimate the power of food. She'd treat us to lunch a couple of times a year and would bring in snacks regularly.

Nancy Denbow, Independent Consultant

A lot of heartache can be headed off at the pass by educating users about what's possible and why. What is the current and planned architecture? What percent of the IS organization is dedicated to "survival" — just keeping the basic systems and data going, not developing new and cool stuff? Often users don't fully understand or appreciate what it takes just to keep the IT doors open, much like IT employees probably don't really appreciate the number of finance professionals it takes to keep the accounting books clean and a paycheck coming to them each week.

The more IT leaders educate themselves about the business, the easier those user expectations are. IT leaders need to encourage "boot camps" and other orientations for their IT professionals who work with the business to help them better understand the business they work with. That means making the time for IT developers and others to be away from their jobs long enough to learn about the businesses they serve.

Jacqueline Meyers, Jostens IS Training

A non-profit corporation with razor-thin margins had been up and running very successfully, in the mid 1970s, using old IBM EAM (punch card) equipment. Then, circa 1976, a slick guy sold them on the idea that they needed to replace their EAM equipment with a more modern IBM System/32. This guy passed himself off as a consultant and sold them on the idea that the System/32, with some custom programming (in RPG II), could take the place of the EAM equipment. However, I don't think he had any real qualifications. In any case, when the time came to cut over to the new system, what do you suppose they did?

At the suggestion of this "consultant," within a few weeks after they began using the new system, a salvage company arrived and tore apart the old EAM equipment for scrap metal. This consultant gave no leadership related to running in parallel for a few days or weeks so that they could validate reports by running the same data on the old machines and the new system and comparing the results. Or if things went really badly, just continuing to use the old system until the bugs could be worked out. Within a short time, it became apparent there were problems, as this company was sending checks to people who owed them money and also sending invoices to people to whom they owed money!

The situation deteriorated rapidly, but the president continued to believe the story of the consultant, who kept promising "we have got it right this time." Within about 18 – 24 months following the implementation of this new system, this company went into Chapter 7 bankruptcy, never to be seen or heard from again. I learned the value of checking for references before trusting a consultant and about a disaster recovery or fall-back plan, in case things don't go according to plan. It was a good lesson to learn early in my career.

Mark Waterbury, Industrial Strength Software

I love your comments on being a servant leader. When I was the team leader for two different software development teams, I tried very hard to take that approach. I felt that my purpose was to be the "enabler" for my team and the one to run "interference" for them. Normally, being an enabler is not a good thing! But I felt my job was to make sure my team could do their jobs efficiently and effectively. So I tried to address and fix the things that stood in their way. Testing going slowly? Would another system help? Yes. So I'd try to find another system to test on. I also tried to take some of the little and the ugly assignments. Each release of the software had us doing a couple of tasks that were tedious. They weren't difficult, but they weren't fun either. Each release, I would take at least one of those ugly tasks. That way, the team could focus on the larger, more interesting projects with fewer distractions.

I felt that my role was not to get work done; rather, it was to make sure my team was able to get their work done.

Also, you alluded to it, but one thing I think any manager/leader has to be able to do — especially a servant leader — is get job satisfaction from helping others accomplish things. I was mentoring a team leader at one of my clients. After several months of trying to be team leader, as well as getting "real" work done, and finally suffering a huge case of burn-out, she came to understand and accept that being a team leader means you don't necessarily get a lot of things done yourself. She's been a "do-er" and a very exceptional do-er at that. But now she's realized that she can't be the effective do-er she once was and be a team leader, too. So I warned her that now she's going to have to get job satisfaction from the fact that her team has accomplished great things — not that she has accomplished great things. I think many IT people are natural do-ers, and being satisfied with accomplishing things through others does not come naturally to most. I think that's why many IT managers still try to "do" — many times to the detriment of the business (because some other part of their duty is being ignored).

Again, you alluded to the fact that you don't have to exert your technical prowess to be a good IT leader. Bit-heads typically make terrible managers and leaders. The "mega-hardware/software" company I used to work for has a "dual" promotion track. That is, you can climb the ranks by taking technical positions, or you can climb the ranks by taking management positions. It used to be that to climb past one point on the technical ladder, you had to cross over and take a management position. Just because the person excels in technology does not mean that they will make a good manager! The percentage of lousy managers dropped significantly when this company dropped the management assignment requirement.

Carol Woodbury, Co-Founder, Skyview Parnters

Two qualities you've espoused are important to bring to light — having business savvy and being a teacher. I had a good friend who was a very technical IT guy who developed a gift over the years for befriending business types. He would mentor them about ways technology could help the business, and he increased their technology vocabularies/understanding. They would help him understand what was going on in the business and help him make better recommendations on how IT could help. It had the additional benefit of him getting to prototype the use of new technologies to see if they would indeed help the business. Tinkering with technology was his passion and a just reward for his enlightened approach.

Brian Fulton, Chief Customer Officer, Executive Velocity Partners

---

When I was a rookie consultant, I found myself in charge of a very important project for a local hospital. The object was to automate the way that therapists did their patient documentation so they could spend more time treating sick kids and less time doing paperwork. It was a big, complicated job, and I dug right in trying to "define the requirements" and get them to tell us what they wanted so we could build it for them. In the middle of a long and frustrating design session with the users, it suddenly struck me that it was even more frustrating for them, because *they did not know what they wanted.*

They didn't know what they wanted because they did not know what was possible or what would be involved in making it happen. What they needed from me was not to religiously copy down what they said, but to help them understand what their choices were and how to make the right decisions. I changed my approach 180 degrees. I stopped "gathering" and started educating. It was a different project from that day on. We made progress, and the users had fun. I have never forgotten that insight. My job is not to do what they want; my job is to help them decide what they should want.

Chris Vaughan, Ph.D., Co-founder, Trillium Solutions Group

Appendix

About the Author

I think it's important to include a little information about what I have done to give you some perspective on why I believe what I do and how I have learned the lessons I have shared.

Robert S. Tipton, Managing Partner, R S Tipton, Incorporated

I have more than 25 years of experience in assisting businesses to develop and implement strategies and technologies designed to transform their organizations. During this time, I have held various roles, including:

- CEO of my own organizational effectiveness and IT consulting business
- CIO of a $1B+ distribution company
- VP/Managing Director for an integrated marketing organization
- VP of corporate capabilities and communications, Global VP of industry technology, and CTO for different professional services firms
- Various positions as developer, designer, project manager, analyst, and development manager spent "in the trenches" developing and supporting IT systems

I am also a popular speaker on both technical and non-technical subjects. I speak each year at numerous conferences and conventions around the world. My speaking style has earned me numerous best-speaker awards for international business groups, conventions, and seminars. My presentations are mostly on effectiveness solutions, including:

- Business transformation
- Organizational development
- Personal effectiveness
- Executive IT awareness and IT planning
- IT strategies
- Networking
- Future technologies

Additionally, for the past 23 years, I have been an active writer and author:

- I have written more than 200 articles.
- I produced a book on database implementations.
- I wrote a chapter for IBM's recent book *The Business Case for e-Business.*
- I have written more than 15 white papers related to IT and business effectiveness issues.
- I have received numerous awards for my writing (including the Award of Achievement and Award of Merit) from the Society for Technical Communications.

Finally, I am a past president of the Institute for Certification of Computing Professionals and a professional member of the National Speakers Association.

Copyright and Graphic Credits

Location	*Name*	*Credit*
Chapter 2	Velveteen Rabbit	Written by Margery Williams Bianco
Chapter 3	Cicso Chart	Yahoo! Finance
Chapter 4	Improvisation	KnAM Theatre, Russia, © 2001, used by permission
	Best Practices	U.S. Centers for Disease Control
	Book image: *Rise of the Creative Class*	Richard Florida, Ph.D., © 2002, used by permission
Chapter 5	Lexus Logo	Registered trademark, Toyota Corp.
	Enron Logo	Registered trademark, Enron Corp.
	Brand experience	MarchFIRST, © 2000
Chapter 6	HR Listens	University of California, San Diego
	Clairvoyance	Magritte, René Francois Ghislain
Chapter 7	Office blueprint	Steve Risley, LLC, © 2002, used by permission
Chapter 9	Miracle Mike	LIFE magazine Oct. 22, 1945, Miracle Mike, the Headless Rooster, Fruita, CO

All other graphics have been used with appropriate licensing agreements and copyrights in place: MS clipart, The Big Box of Art, Hemera Technologies, R S Tipton, Incorporated.

Robert S. Tipton: Make Contact

*E*ffectiveness is not always measured in quarters on the calendar. Sometimes effectiveness takes a long-term, unwavering commitment. The bristlecone pine measures its effectiveness by its ability to thrive for centuries, often amid the harshest and most inhospitable weather conditions. Nature has prepared the tree well for the challenges it will face in its life.

However, when it comes to finding help with personal effectiveness in working and real-life situations, we're often at a loss about what to do. Unfortunately, we too often take wrong turns and waste time chasing blind alleys.

R S Tipton's Effectiveness Solutions mix common sense, out-of-the-box thinking, personal advocacy, and purposeful challenging of the status quo to create extraordinary results. If you are a success-motivated person, looking to make significant steps forward in your business, with your IT department, or in your real-life situations, **R S Tipton's Effectiveness Solutions** may be right for you.

R S Tipton, Incorporated
1041 W. Dry Creek Road • Littleton, CO • 80120
303.797.0180 • www.rstipton.com